To Beth

NEVER

work with

CHILDREN OR ANIMALS

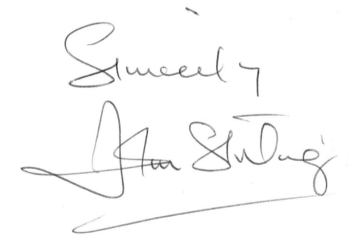

Sincerely

Stan Stirling

Previous works by John Stirling:

Marked for Life (BBC)

Underdogs

Not One Bray Goes By

Gert and Daisy

Cheers Mrs Worthington

Lowry, the Concert

Dot Cotton's Masterclass on Donizetti

Once in a Lifetime

NEVER

work with

CHILDREN OR ANIMALS

by John Stirling

with Chris Newton

MEMOIRS

Cirencester

Published by Memoirs

MEMOIRS

AUTOBIOGRAPHIES
& FAMILY HISTORIES

25 Market Place
Cirencester Gloucestershire
GL7 2NX

Copyright © John Stirling, March 2010
First published in England, March 2010

Book jacket design Ray Lipscombe

ISBN 978-0-9565 102-0-4

Printed in England

For Annie

"When you reach the top of the hill, look over your shoulder
and you will see what you have achieved"

John

Acknowledgments

I would like to thank the following for their contributions to this book, and to my life:

June Brown MBE, for being a wonderful president and a great friend.

Dame Judi Dench and Michael Williams, for their continued support.

Sir John Mills and Hayley Mills, for making so many wonderful things happen.

Sir Robin Janvrin, for our royal encounter.

Patricia Hayes OBE, for a lifelong friendship and some of the wisest advice.

Bill Kenwright CBE, for making things happen and for his generosity and care.

Michael Denison CBE, for believing in me when everything was going down and helping to put it all together again.

Michael Elliott OBE, for giving me the opportunities and the direction.

Jenny Seagrove, for her love of animals and the help she gives them.

Peter Smith, past chairman of the Trust, who put me on the straight and narrow.

Arnold Fear, our treasurer, for doing a difficult job so well.

Elaine Walker, my very able accountant.

Phil and Alisa Rogers, the most generous benefactors, who saw me and the donkeys through the worst winter ever.

Julie Homewood, whose creative input has always been a huge help, and for her cheerful voice on the end of the phone.

Rolf Harris, a friend, a colleague, a campaigner for animals and a joy to children and adults alike.

Billy Fury, a truly spectacular man and a great friend.

Ian and Arlene Huzzard, solid friends and Trustees.

Elizabeth Heneker JP, a very genuine friend and an enormous help to us both.

Chris Newton of Memoirs Books, for bringing this story to life by rearranging my troubled and long-winded ramblings so that they made sense.

Last but not least, Eric Morecambe - the man who gave me strength, confidence and friendship and who pushed to get through the boundaries and opened many doors.

And of course - my family.

John Stirling, March 2010

Dedication

I have decided to dedicate this book to a fellow producer – Bill Kenwright CBE. Bill and I do not know each other particularly well, but our lives have followed similar paths and our shared devotion to the theatre has forged a common bond between us over many years. Like me, Bill started out as a young actor before turning his attention to producing. Over the years he has inspired me in countless ways. His loyalty to and love of the arts are unmatched (except perhaps by his devotion to Everton, the team he serves as chairman). Through his own troubled years of personal hardship and sacrifice, despite having far less support than he deserved, he forged on with extraordinary determination – and he is still forging on. Bill and I both served long and arduous apprenticeships based on nothing more substantial than our belief in our own raw talent. Yet however hard it might all have seemed at the time, I hope this effort of mine will reinforce his belief that the old days really were the good days. Bill's generosity towards friends and colleagues, both privately and publicly, elevate him to the very topmost ranks of our profession. His kindness is remarkable, and his help and encouragement for me personally have been invaluable. In 2002 I was very proud to present Bill with the Michael Elliott Trust Award for Producer of the Year. We have many talented producers working in the theatre today, but Bill, I believe, is the only one to merit the title 'impresario'.

So Bill - here's to you.

John Stirling

Introduction

John Stirling followed his parent's footsteps into a theatrical career while he was still in short trousers. He became a successful child actor on TV and radio in the golden days of the 1950s and 60s before embarking on a varied and colourful career backstage, and sometimes upon it. As a producer or stage manager, John has worked with everyone from Bob Monkhouse and Morecambe and Wise to the Beatles, Billy Fury, Marti Caine and Mark Knopfler, and put on variety shows for good causes in the country's biggest theatres and concert halls. He has worked as a stage manager on *Coronation Street*, talent-spotted for prime-time TV programmes and created a new-look Gang Show.

John's life changed for ever in 1989 when he and his wife Annie were moved by pity to rescue two abused and battered donkeys from a horse sale. John and Annie went on to create a sanctuary for the animals and others like them which now, under the auspices of the Michael Elliott Trust, is home to the best part of two hundred donkeys.

Since donkeys galloped into his life, John has directed all his show-business skills to raising money for his charges and for the Trust. In this he has enlisted the help of a galaxy of famous figures, from Dame Judi Dench to Chris de Burgh and from June Brown, Rolf Harris and Pam Ayres to late Sir John Mills. He is able to count many of Britain's greatest stars of stage and screen as his friends.

This book tells the story of John's life in the entertainment business, and of the events that led to his taking up the donkeys' cause.

Foreword

I well remember the surprise when I took a call on the *EastEnders* set one day from John Stirling. I remembered him from the early 1960s, when John had been a boy actor working on *Dixon of Dock Green* with my late husband Robert Arnold. Robert always used to say what a good young actor John was, but now it seemed he was high up the ranks of television producers.

John told me that he was in the process of starting a donkey sanctuary, and asked if I could help by giving a special concert performance of a production called *Dot Cotton's Masterclass on Donizetti* at the enchanting Buxton Opera House as part of the Buxton Festival. When he told me that the money raised from the show would enable him to get his project off the ground, I was delighted to accept his invitation.

I have now been President of the Trust for more than 20 years, and my admiration for John and Annie Stirling and their achievement in creating the sanctuary and the trust cannot be expressed in words. It is not just the donkeys who have benefited, but many delightful children with special needs.

I hope that when you have read this book you will agree with me that John and Annie are two unique and phenomenally courageous people.

June Brown
President, the Michael Elliott Trust

A message from Dame Judi Dench

This remarkable account of a life in theatre, variety and television is unique. I have always found John and his work fun and inspiring, and here we have a record for our archives of just how good those times were.

John certainly is now what he was and always will be – great fun.

Judi Dench

Contents

Chapter 1

The boy born in a hamper

I have never really understood why I was expelled from my first school at the tender age of 10. I take consolation in the fact that in today's world, such a decision would have been properly reviewed, and very likely reversed. I know such drastic action is sometimes the only option in these days of assaults on teachers, vicious bullying, burning schools down – even murder. But my crime back in 1954 seems to have been simply that I liked letting off steam by singing and dancing rather more than the study of algebra and the history of the Roman Empire.

"Jean-Pierre Richer does not consider his academic future with any importance or urgency" read the report from the Lycée Française du Royaume Uni (yes, I have it still). "He cannot walk from one classroom to another or down a corridor without breaking into a song and dance routine, which is very disruptive and often leads to the rest of his class following suit, disrupting discipline and enticing behaviour of an unruly manner... We feel it is in both the child's and the school's interest that he is found a different educational establishment to continue his advancement, one more suited to his needs and disposition. He has always kept good time and been polite, but that is not all that is required!"

No doubt the *Lycée* saw in me a delinquent coming of age. I was made painfully aware that I was the first boy either in the school or in my family to have such a stigma attached to me.

1

Chapter 1

My mother, Pamela Stirling, was an actress of some fame – she was a Rank starlet of great accomplishment, both in Britain and in France. Appropriately to her calling, she insisted on creating a three-act drama out of my fall from grace. She was as uncompromising and furious with me as she was with the school.

My father, Gaston Richer, was an opera singer who had fought a hard war; he had been taken prisoner twice and incarcerated in prisons as far away as Russia. He must have been a resourceful man, because with five brave comrades he managed to escape and make his way back home to France.

I never did find out how he managed this, as he never spoke about it. But his experiences did not damage his love of life and of singing, and we would hear his voice day and night around the house. He would sing from *The Barber of Seville* and at bedtime it would be *La Bohème*, or at any rate three of its best-known arias. So perhaps it was hardly surprising that I too liked to sing and dance from an early age.

After the little episode with the French school we wasted no time in moving away. Initially we bought a house in Chelsea, but this still wasn't quite far enough away for my mother, so we moved out to rural Putney.

At last I no longer had to endure the jeering as I passed the school railings. Yet I would gain solace from the looks on my former schoolmates' faces – I, after all, was the one on the outside, the one who had gained his freedom. They still had another six years to serve.

Something had to be done about me, and quickly, so that my mother could recover her image and her self-respect and so that I could get on with my life with some vestige of personal dignity - along with the more practical matter of qualifying for some sort of career. The answer to it all was staring us in the face; the stage.

Chapter 1

My father was reluctant to recognise this as my destiny, but my mother liked to think she had spawned a great talent which was waiting only for the opportunity to burst out on an unsuspecting public.

My mother had had the distinction of being the first English actress to star in the Comédie Française. She appeared in films with James Mason and John Mills, among others, and was tremendously respected on both sides of the Channel. She was also very beautiful. My grandfather, Edward Stirling, and my grandmother, Margaret Vaughan, had been well known for their touring theatre the English Players. They travelled the world for many years, playing in all to 122 countries. They brought their own brands of plays in English to countries which had never heard of such masterpieces as *Journey's End*, *Pygmalion* and *An Inspector Calls*.

My father's greatest moment of fame arrived in 1953 when he was cast in *The Cruel Sea* alongside Jack Hawkins, Donald Sinden, Denholm Elliott, Bryan Forbes and Virginia McKenna. He played the part of a French captain who was rescued from the ocean by Captain Ericson, played by Jack Hawkins. Shooting this episode meant eight days' filming in a freezing cold-water tank at Ealing studios, immersed up to his waist from eight in the morning to eight at night. The other actors did not realise that under his costume Dad was wearing a corset to enable him to recover from a slipped disc. He never let on how much pain he was in.

Dad was hospitalised after the filming, and while he was recuperating his agent did a bunk with his fee for the film, so he never got a penny for all his valiant efforts.

Though my father was a fine actor, singing was always his first love. Each year I would be taken to the Odeon in Leicester Square, where he would perform for the Free French Association and ex-fighters from the French Resistance, of which he had been very much a part during the war years.

Chapter 1

There was talent with the pen in my family, too – my aunt, Monica Stirling, was a best-selling writer whose books included a work about Napoleon's mother called *The Pride of Lions* and a biography of Hans Christian Andersen, *The Wild Swan*. Aunt Monica never fully recovered from her experiences at the end of the war, when she had to accompany the American liberation forces into the concentration camps. She was then a reporter for *Life* magazine, and the sights she confronted lived on with her for the rest of her life.

My grandmother would introduce me to everyone as 'the boy born in a hamper', a term often used in the theatrical world for the offspring of actors. I soon started to have an identity crisis, thanks to a baffling experience which I had to undergo each time I was taken to see my mother in a play. She would take me backstage and introduce me to the rest of the cast as her nephew. My grandmother tried to explain to me that this was because young actresses in the West End had to be very careful about admitting how old they were. An actress's age was considered secret. If she was known to have a child as old as I was it would be assumed she had been through life's mill. She might be suitable for the more mature parts, but not the romantic leads.

The obvious course was for everyone to pretend that I was someone else. My mother did, after all, look far too young and beautiful to have a child of my age. It didn't help, however, that I happened to look a great deal like her, which tended to bring us some old-fashioned looks. Looking back, I suppose you could say that the role of Pamela Stirling's nephew was my introduction to acting.

The first step was for me to attend an audition at the Italia Conti Academy, the country's foremost stage school. My mother was far from convinced that I would make it, but she bravely laid her gremlins to rest for the day, deposited her 'nephew' with friends and came with me as my mother for

Chapter 1

once, gritting her teeth and praying that no-one would see us.

Fortunately I was accepted straight away. It seemed that I had been given an opportunity to show everybody what I was capable of, given the chance.

The principal, Miss Ruth Conti, had only one reservation – my name. As Jean-Pierre Richer I would be assumed to be French, and might not be accepted for English parts. Miss Conti suggested that I take my mother's name, and so it was that overnight, still only 10 years old, I became John Stirling.

This was a little confusing. I was John Stirling at school, Hercule the naughty nephew at night (the name my grandmother used for me, which I hated) and Jean-Pierre when my father was around (we did not want to upset him or his family). Yet my father gave his full approval to my stage name. In fact, he went one better - by divorcing my mother.

This was not such a shock as it may sound. I knew that by now both my parents had formed partnerships with other people with whom they wanted to spend their lives, and the split was all very amicable. However, I did miss my father terribly when he set sail for France. and after that heart-rending break we never managed to regain our fondness for each other.

So I entered the portals of the Italia Conti Academy with a new name, a new satchel, a new season ticket and a new lunchbox, along with new tights, tap shoes, ballet shoes and uniform. I did keep the old beret which had protected my head during the years at the French school, and was outraged when Augustine, our Dutch au pair, threw it out a few months later. Augustine never managed to get back on my good side after that, and I'm afraid I did my best to make life difficult for her. She used to cook red cabbage every day, making it into all sorts of 'delicacies' which both my new stepfather and I detested. It wasn't long before she went back to Holland.

Chapter 1

I still chuckle at the memory of that beret, and in particular how funny the bullies at the Lycée found it when I suffered a bout of ringworm. How they would laugh when they whipped it off my head to reveal my bald pate, shaved and painted mauve with ringworm lotion. And how different their expressions were a few days later when it was their turn to sport purple heads, for they soon found out how contagious ringworm was.

It was my ability to make people smile which made my teachers aware that I had a penchant in that direction. Some sort of personality was emerging from within, and one that I was ready to share with everyone. I was certainly never short of words. Sometimes this worked against me, but more often than not it acted to break the ice with strangers and made me seem interesting enough to be noticed.

I showed ability in the tap-dancing classes, though my ballet technique left something to be desired, not helped by the horror of having to appear in tights in public. Most of my schoolmates tried to stifle their mirth at my thin and bandy legs, their shape accentuated by the tights. I was dubbed Butterball, I presume because of my resemblance to a supermarket chicken.

My singing teacher was Helen Vokes, an enthusiastic lady of 70. Mrs Vokes' most striking attribute was her extraordinarily long fingernails - all you could hear as she accompanied your chosen piece was the clatter of her nails on the ivories. But I have Mrs Vokes to thank for the encouragement she gave me for my singing. She told me I had a fine natural voice with a good range, which spurred me on to do better.

Years later all this singing, dancing and acting would be responsible for my entering a side of the entertainment business which back then I never knew existed. For now, I had to concentrate on my apprenticeship - and start a new life as a child actor.

*Grandmother Margaret Vaughan
(above and below)*

Mother Pamela playing Joan of Arc, with her father Edward

Father in Journey's End

Pamela Stirling as the young Queen Victoria in an early BBC production

Pamela & baby John

John & Pills

Pamela and Gaston on their wedding day

Never content to follow the herd – a young John (far right) at the Lycee

A carthorse in the shed

No. 45 Howards Lane was a desirable two-storey five-bedroomed house in the leafy suburb of Putney, SW15. For the first time in my life, we had a garden. The garden had a shed, and we hadn't lived there very long before it became a home in its own right - to my pets.

First it was Dutch rabbits. I forgot to separate the sexes, a mistake which left me with fewer rabbits rather than more because the female ate the male (I hadn't read my animal encyclopaedia properly). There were hamsters which bred for England, followed by white mice which made the hamsters look celibate by comparison. The local pet shop looked after me very well. So they should have, considering how much money they were making out of me.

Around this time my mother remarried - to another Frenchman, Claude Le Saché, a BBC World Service producer. Claude had his own programme which was transmitted daily to France from Bush House in London. Every day he had to write, produce and present a 30-minute show - quite a challenge, but he managed it very successfully. Claude was studious, professional, hardworking and generous, and I liked him very much.

I was grateful that he never tried to take the place of my father. Sensitive to the issue, my mother quickly produced a daughter for him, Marie-Victoire, and we all got on very well indeed.

Now that my grandfather had passed on, my grandmother also lived with us - something else that suited me very well. We were a happy family.

Until Claude spoilt everything. I had found a large and rather fat piebald carthorse called Pills, who desperately needed a home. I suggested to my mother that Pills would make a much more interesting pet than mice and hamsters and that our potting shed would make the perfect stable for him. I was deeply hurt by Claude's suggestion that Pills would not even be able to get into our garden shed, let alone live there in comfort.

"How will we know if we don't even try?" I pleaded, producing a flood of tears on cue (I was, after all, now a pupil at the finest drama school in the country).

"Where would we put the washing machine?" replied Claude. "What would we do with all the muck?"

As if such matters were of any importance! And who was this newcomer to lay down the rules in MY house anyway?

"We could put it on the flowers" I suggested.

"You mean those little flower boxes? Don't you think they would collapse under the weight?"

Now he was trying to be funny! I withdrew into a long sulk. From the security of my bedroom I sent Claude a series of pleading notes with maps of Wimbledon Common, Putney Common and the bridle paths around Roehampton and Richmond Park fields, pointing out how well all this open country would suit Pills. Claude's replies were polite but firm and of course, I lost the battle.

The episode did, however, wake my family up to my budding love of horses. It also gave Claude an idea, such a good one that I quickly forgave him. He found a wonderful riding school, Stocklands in Petersfield,

Hampshire, and suggested I spend my school holidays in residence there, learning to ride properly and work with horses. They would even take Pills along with his owner.

That was the beginning of the greatest happiness of my life. For three years, until Pills died peacefully one September day, I shared my Easter and summer holidays with him at Stocklands. My memories of all those wonderful, quiet times together have outweighed all the successes I have enjoyed in my working life. It was through Pills too that I met my first donkey. Violetta shared his sanctuary, and we quickly became close friends. I didn't know it at the time, but she and others of her kind were to play a big part in my life.

The Italia Conti Stage School had one drawback; it was slap in the middle of London's red light district. Number 12 Archer Street Soho was directly behind the Windmill Theatre, with its nude shows and its slogan 'we never close'. The school was flanked on all sides by brothels, massage parlours and seedy barber shops which advertised more than just a short back and sides. The two local theatres had nowhere to promote their shows - Sid the Barber seemed to be using every available billboard to advertise condoms. Many of the doorways along Archer Street were permanently open, with a single light bulb illuminating the foot of a carpetless stairway to heaven. The cards on the doors left little to the imagination. 'Gloria can do it for you!' 'Denise just can't say no!' 'Emma is amiable!' they read, and, much to my surprise, 'Auntie Nelly has the experience you're looking for!' I always hoped to meet the enigmatic Auntie Nellie, but I never did; perhaps she took to disguise when out on the street.

The ladies of the night were just as busy during the day. I couldn't imagine where they got their energy. After a tap class, a ballet class a singing class I would be completely exhausted. How could Auntie Nellie carry on offering her mysterious 'experiences' day and night?

Chapter 2

The girls were a cheery bunch. They would lean out of their windows and shout at us students each morning as we arrived for assembly. "What've you got in your lunchbox, dearie?" they would call, or "Wish your dad a happy Christmas from me!".

In the evenings as we left for home, the messages were more sombre. "You take care, kids" or "Get home safely!" they would call, and it was all received in the kind spirit in which it was intended. They kept an eye on us, even to the extent of knowing when one of us was off sick or away working. Ironically those girls helped to make Soho a safe community.

The stage door of the Windmill Theatre was right opposite the school. In the warmer months the girls would take their breaks out there from their 12-shows-a-day routine or pop out for a fag between scenes. They were often draped in nothing but a scanty towel or two, which for boys reaching puberty was rather hard to take, if you'll forgive the expression.

A few of the girls had actually trained at Italia Conti themselves, and we would use that as our excuse to nip over the road and have a chat - about theatrical matters, naturally!

The girls loved the attention and were very kind to us. We would ask them about their time at the school and be invited to take a few puffs on their cigarettes. Many boys who had no intention of taking up smoking would make an exception on these occasions.

I found that Sid the Barber had a kindly side. If I travelled into town with Claude, who was in the habit of making a 5.30 start, I would arrive a couple of hours early. At this time of day Sid would be busy attending to his tattoo clients, and he would allow me to wait in the comfort and security of the shop while I waited for school to start. I didn't much enjoy having to watch overweight middle-aged men bending over the arm of his barber's chair with their trousers round their ankles as Sid drilled the ink

10

into their more private areas, but at least I was safe, warm and dry.

Italia Conti was an exclusive school; that year there were just 32 pupils, 14 boys and 18 girls. Naturally I got used to wearing tights, sometimes with leg warmers or knee-length socks. One day we left our jockstraps off for comfort. Deep was our embarrassment when the Windmill girls noticed our all-too-obvious delight at their charms. After that we made sure the jockstraps stayed on.

It wasn't long before we started to get our first working assignments. The little money we were paid naturally all went towards my school fees. My performance in the academic subjects made it clear to the teaching staff that I should concentrate on my theatrical career.

Many of the children at the school, though far more talented than me, suffered so badly from their nerves that their real talent would fail to come through at auditions. It didn't help that they were often put under excessive pressure from their parents to do well. I was lucky. I never suffered from nerves and was easy to direct; I was polite and respectful and most directors found they could get a good performance out of me without too much effort. The roles began to come in.

My mother was very pleased to be able to talk of me to her friends with pride at last. My parents always wished me well and had my best interests at heart, but they never came to my auditions and very rarely to my performances. That may sound odd, but it was fine by me. They were pros, and they knew that the stage was just a job. Make sure you're word perfect, they would say; do your best to get it right and please the audience - and then come home and forget about it. If it all went pear-shaped they would take me to one side and tell me where I must have gone wrong - and I listened. I knew I needed their advice, and I was grateful for it. I still am.

At the end of each year the school would put on a special show. It had two aims; to keep eager parents abreast of the progress their offspring had made, and at the same time to show us off to casting agents and producers in search of new talent. We would present a scene from one of Shakespeare's plays and then, to show our versatility, perform a song-and-dance routine.

In 1956, when I was 12, the chosen play was *Hamlet*. Each boy had to team up with one of the girls to learn and perform a scene. There were 14 girls and only 11 boys that year, so some of the boys had to perform twice.

When we studied the notice board to see who we'd been teamed with, I was delighted to see that I had been put with Anne Rogers. Anne was an extremely attractive blonde with a trim figure and a very pretty face and a lovely personality to go with it. That year she was very much the school pinup, and her photos adorned the boys' changing room.

My regular companion that year, a sweet girl called Rochelle O'Berman, was not quite so enthusiastic about this. Salt was rubbed into Rochelle's wound when Miss Conti cast Rochelle as the gravedigger - scarcely the most glamorous role for a girl. I did my best to persuade Rochelle that this was a great opportunity to show what she could do, but she was not convinced.

The chosen scene was one where Ophelia was in her bedroom and Hamlet is showing his advancing delusion, paranoia and schizophrenia. At that time the play was running at the Old Vic, so Miss Conti decided to take us to see it done properly. John Neville was playing Hamlet, while the part of Ophelia had been given to an up-and-coming young actress called Judi Dench.

It was an outing I will never forget. I still remember the hushed atmosphere as we waited for the curtain to rise, and the smell of size from the backcloths - a fragrance all theatre people learn to recognise.

Chapter 2

John Neville gave a marvellous performance, but for us the star was Judi Dench. She did not seem much older than us, yet she was in a different league from anything we had seen before. We found her mesmerising, spellbinding, youthful and beautiful. The girls were a little intimidated by her, wondering, as well they might, how they could ever hope to follow such a performance. We boys, on the other hand, just fell in love with her.

The next day our new heroine's picture was hoisted high above the coat racks and lockers in the boys' changing room. Judi's performance was an inspiration that has stayed with me to this day.

Chapter 3

Whacko!

My first break in television came when a Scottish director called Douglas Moodie cast me in the BBC situation comedy series *Whacko!*. Written by Frank Muir and Denis Norden, it starred Jimmy Edwards as the headmaster of Chislebury School for Boys.

The team had searched high and low for a small boy who could play the lead role of Lumley. Frank and Denis told me afterwards that my honesty about having been expelled from my first school had clinched it for me!

The other leading boy, Taplow, was played by John Hall. Taplow had brains, and would outwit the headmaster with intelligence and cunning. Lumley, on the other hand, was a little short of common sense and would cause constant disruptions.

Jimmy Edwards wasn't just a very clever and accomplished comedian - he was a genuine professor with a successful teaching career behind him. And Jimmy and I had something in common - the Windmill Theatre, where he had appeared regularly after the war, 'dying with the best of them twelve times a day' as he put it. He would tell us how difficult he found it trying to crack jokes to the men in the front row with their blank stares and their mackintoshes over their laps, but it was, as he said, the best apprenticeship in the world.

I greatly admired Frank Muir and Denis Norden. We would broadcast the show live at the Shepherd's Bush theatre in front of an audience of

500, and before each performance they would perform a warm-up spot. Their introductions were so funny that we found them a hard act to follow.

Because the show was live, making mistakes or forgetting our lines was unthinkable. Jimmy was very clever at covering up when something went wrong. Every object on his desk had his lines written on them, just in case. Once the phone rang - Jimmy tried to answer it, only to find that the prop man had forgotten to put a phone on the set. He went straight into a hilarious comedy routine, pretending to look for it. After that it was quite a job to get back to the script. I adored him, and learned an awful lot from him over the four years I played Lumley.

Pettigrew, the bumbling assistant headmaster, was beautifully played by Arthur Howard, brother of the actor Leslie Howard. Arthur and Jimmy made a wonderful team. Liz Frazer played the matron. She was such fun and so sweet that I quickly fell for her.

One morning during rehearsals, Douglas Moodie came over to ask me if I would take a part in the BBC TV series *Dixon of Dock Green*. He was directing both shows in the same rehearsal rooms at the Acton Boys' Club, *Whacko!* on the ground floor in the mornings and *Dixon* upstairs in the afternoons.

I spent many months doing the two shows in parallel. This was a more serious part, that of a boy in trouble with the police, which I felt would stretch me a little more as an actor.

I used to go home with a chaperone, usually my grandmother, on the bus. After the first couple of episodes of *Whacko!* were broadcast I was amazed to find that people would recognise me. The conductor actually asked for my autograph. At the shops, people would come up to me and talk as if they knew me - quite extraordinary. In the persona of Lumley I was asked to open shops and fêtes, even to visit schools. I was grateful for Lumley's

Chapter 3

horn-rimmed spectacles - once I had taken them off I was a little harder to recognise in the street.

My next part came about because of my French background. A TV director called Michael Elliott picked me to play a young boy in a play called *Marjolaine,* which was based on a true story. My character, known as the Rabbit, was used by the French Resistance to infiltrate the Germans and pass on valuable information through a labyrinth of tunnels.

This was a big part. The play was a 90-minute production, and once again we were broadcasting live. Michael Elliott was a superb director who took enormous time and effort to help me. Most directors disappear into the control room high in the ceiling of the studio - not Michael. He directed the whole play by lodging himself on Camera 1's ledge and being transported with the camera to each scene. To know he was there and was seeing everything was very comforting.

I was able to meet the real Rabbit when he came over from France for the previews; he was in his thirties by then. He said, very kindly, that he thought I had got very near to the real thing.

Marjolaine was a big hit. Michael went on to direct another production called *Mrs Wickens in the Fall,* the story of an elderly American couple who adopt a young boy in London, and I was given the part of the boy. The production earned Michael his first Emmy Award.

After all this fame and glory, it was time for a twelve-year-old to come back to earth. I returned to school for a while to catch up on my schoolwork. I did have tutors on the sets, but it's not the same as being with your mates at school. You miss the fun and the companionship, even the schoolwork. I managed to pass some dance exams and ballet grades, and my singing lessons went well.

Chapter 3

But it wasn't long before I was back at the BBC. This time it was a Charles Dickens series, and I was given junior parts in *Our Mutual Friend*, *The Old Curiosity Shop* and finally *Nicholas Nickleby* - once again, all broadcast live.

It was quite a treat going for fittings at Maurice Angel's and having wonderful costumes and wigs made. The hours in make-up were a revelation. I was given an assortment of warts, a false nose, various scars and false cheeks, a hunchback, braces, even jaw extensions - it was all great fun.

But the real treat was the cast. I worked alongside people like Patrick Troughton, Patricia Hayes, Eric Porter, Denholm Elliott, Esmond Knight, William Russell and Liz Smith - all household names for many years (Liz retired only in 2009, at the age of 87), and all wonderful character actors who really knew how to bring the scripts to life. In company like that, giving a good performance was easy.

I did have a difficult moment in one scene. I was playing Quilp's clerk, sitting on a very high stool with a desk in front of me and quills and parchment papers all around. Patrick Troughton looked terrifying as Quilp, and I wasn't too pretty a sight myself.

Then Esmond Knight walked in. We had rehearsed the scene all week, but now something was different. Knight had lost an eye in active service during the war. For the sake of authenticity, without warning anyone, he had decided to remove his glass eye before the scene.

As I spoke the opening line, Esmond's back was turned. Then he turned round and stared at me. I saw the gaping eye-socket - and froze.

Patrick leapt into the ghastly silence and carried the scene forward. I managed to recover, but it had been a terrifying experience. Esmond apologised afterwards, explaining that he thought it would add tension to the scene. It certainly did that. When I got home, my mother said it had been one of the highlights of the episode.

My grandmother had found her vocation in life as my chaperone. She knew most of the actors and actresses personally and loved to chat to them. 'Nookie', as we called her, always treated me as an adult and a professional actor. What a woman she was.

Michael Elliott now came up with a production that would change my life. He cast me as Pipeto in *A Small Miracle*, the story of a young boy who persuades the Pope to allow him to take his sick donkey to the crypt of St Francis to make it better. The story first saw the light of day as a film called *Never Take No For An Answer*, which I knew well - I had seen it many times in the cinema with my mother and a box of Kleenex close at hand. I was extremely worried about undertaking the part after this boy's success. I knew that to follow his performance would be impossible. I would do most things for Michael, but not this. He would have to find another boy.

Michael could see my point. He was shaken that one so young had seen the sense in turning down the role.

But none of this was helping my education. Ruth Conti stepped in. I had done an unprecedented 400 television appearances in four years. It was time to get back to work.

For a while I returned to the classroom, but it was increasingly clear that I was never going to achieve anything there. My teacher, Miss Mulvey, had had enough of my refusal to learn.

The BBC stepped in again. I was asked to join the BBC Repertory Drama Company (Radio). Can you imagine how it felt at fourteen to become the first child actor allowed into the Inner Sanctum?

Chapter 3

I played all the children's parts, from the *Princes in the Tower* to Jennings the schoolboy. It was all quite wonderful.

Some moments live on in the mind forever. One year the BBC decided to embark on a full-scale production of Nicolai's opera *The Merry Wives of Windsor*. It was to be that year's flagship programme for the corporation.

They brought over the much revered operatic director George Foa. Foa was a gentle but authoritative man with a trail of operatic successes all over the world. His innovative approach had made him very much sought after. He flew in the world-famous Spanish soprano Victoria de Los Angeles to take the lead and built a large supporting cast around her, with some of the world's most renowned opera stars.

George made some startling decisions. His first move was to announce that he would shoot the whole thing in the grounds of Windsor Great Park. His next was to house his 90-piece concert orchestra in the Riverside Studios in Hammersmith, a full 20 miles away. Third, just to make things even more difficult for the sound boys, he placed the 200-strong chorus in the Lime Grove Studios in Shepherd's Bush.

On top of all this, the opera was to be transmitted live! The stars, however, recorded their parts beforehand. The voices would never have come over strongly enough on location, and the audience could hardly be expected to take seriously the spectacle of a soprano singing a strenuous aria while doing a four-minute mile across the park.

Although they were miming the singers still needed to see the conductor, so they had monitors following them around showing him on the rostrum. The chorus however were not so lucky in their dungeon in Shepherd's Bush, and had to rely on a wing and a prayer and the sound of the orchestra.

Chapter 3

For me, this was the greatest job yet. I played Victoria de Los Angeles' page. I had no lines to remember. All I had to do was leap and cavort around the bushes and hedges, up trees and in and out of rivers and generally career at high speed around Windsor Great Park.

In tights, of course. Bright yellow this time.

Despite all the challenges, against all the odds, George Foa pulled off the production. It was a miracle of production technology.

Chapter 4

Radio days

My prefect at school was Anthony Newley. He was working for his ticket, as it were. A very talented young actor, he was dragging himself up from a background of poverty. Ruth Conti saw the potential of this strange but extremely talented young man and set up a scholarship to enable him to work with the students while studying, and perhaps get some work from the school's casting agency. The head girl was a young redhead called Millicent Martin.

Anthony was quite brilliant. His approach to his work was entirely original. Having thoroughly learned a part, he would reassemble it into something entirely fresh.

I still listen to his records with joy. I would go each week to see his West End musical *Stop The World, I Want To Get Off,* and sit mesmerised by his talent.

One of my early radio broadcasts for the BBC Repertory Company was the role of the elder of two brothers in a detective story. The younger brother was played by Patricia Hayes. Patricia specialised in children's voices, and she was very convincing. She studied children a great deal and had three of her own she could model her voices on.

Patricia supported pretty much all our top comics, yet she was equally accomplished as a serious actress; her performance in *Edna the Inebriate Woman* (1971) is still well remembered. Even on radio, Patricia would make all the gestures along with the words. None of the rest of us dared to do this for fear of losing our places or dropping our scripts, but she had none of those worries. As my 'brother', she would hug me and cuddle me as the script suggested. Patricia was the most generous and gracious of actresses and we became close friends.

When I got the part of Ernie Bluett in Ted Ray's series *Ray's a Laugh,* Patricia was visibly upset - she had hoped to get the part herself. After the last episode had gone out, she handed me an envelope and left without a word. When I got back to my dressing-room, there she was. I opened the envelope.

"I am so glad you played Ernie Bluett" it said. "I have enjoyed every single episode. You have done a terrific job and been able to bring a new dimension to the series which it needed. Although I make my living mimicking children's voice there really can never be any substitute for the real thing and you have proved that to me you have incredible comedy timing for one so young. My love & thanks, Pat x". We have never had a cross word since then.

My next venture was an adventure series called *Paco Bayes,* set in Spain, though it was filmed at Ealing Studios. At the auditions there was a lengthy debate about the casting of Paco.

"Would you consider playing Paco?" asked the producer, Richard West. To his surprise I didn't immediately accept.

"On one condition" I said. Everything went deadly quiet.

"A small Spanish village in the middle of nowhere would have a donkey to do all the work" I went on. "I would like my Violetta with me for the series. She's a donkey."

I got the part, and Violetta and I had a marvellous twelve weeks together.

Chapter 4

I was now sixteen years old and after the Paco series I felt the days of juvenile roles were probably over for me. I did one more sitcom, *Taxi*, with the great Sid James. I played a drummer in a group; two of the other members of the group were Steve Marriott and Rod Stewart, who both became pop stars in their own right. It was great fun, and gave me a taste for the pop world.

I asked the BBC if I could buy the drum kit I'd been using - I was delighted when they gave it to me for nothing. It was a full professional drum kit, all packed into individual flight cases. When I set it up at the top of the house it took up practically the whole room.

For the sake of the rest of the household my mother was swift to impose some rules - no practising before 11 am, after 4 pm or on Sundays, and no more than 90 minutes a day. I took a course at Wimbledon Music College. I had problems reading music, but I persevered.

One Thursday I noticed an advertisement in *The Stage* for a drummer to accompany organist Handel Evans for a 26-week summer season at the Spa Pavilion in Felixstowe. It had been placed by Harry and Marjorie Ristori from the Grand Order of Water Rats. I knew Harry and Marjorie, so I got in touch. They gave me the job.

That summer 1961 engagement in Felixstowe gave me a chance to take a rest from acting and concentrate on the music I loved. I left Italia Conti that summer with three GCE passes, which was three more than some feared I would get. I felt dreadfully sad at leaving the school which had meant so much to me. There were many goodbyes and quite a few tears, not just from my schoolmates but from Sid the barber, the lovely Windmill girls, the ladies of the night in their window seats, even the conductress on the no. 14 bus.

I spent the week that followed sitting at our kitchen table, head in hands, barely speaking to anyone. The world had become a sad and gloomy place.

But this wasn't just a temporary sense of anti-climax. I felt that, almost as soon as it had begun, my career as an actor was over. The mere idea of somehow trying to transform myself into a juvenile or romantic lead frightened me to death. Those wonderful years playing everything from Noddy to the Dauphin in *Saint Joan* had, quite frankly, burned me out.

The prospect of my season in Felixstowe cheered me up. My grandmother remembered that her friend Megs Jenkins, the character actress, had invested her capital in a large sea-front hotel there which was due to open that summer. She took the train to Felixstowe and paid Megs a visit. Megs did have a few concerns about the likely behaviour of a 16-year-old newly let loose on the world, but Nookie soon talked her round and persuaded her to accept a very modest £6 a week for my board and lodging.

The hotel was a splendid place - I think it was called the Mandalay. Photographs of Megs' past theatrical triumphs were displayed on all the staircases, while her awards glittered on the landing. Her fame and charm made a great impression on her guests, while her Italian partner's superb cooking ensured happiness in the dining room. Most of my fellow performers would be content with a parcel of fish and chips for their evening meal but I had a three-course, cordon bleu dinner - not bad on six quid a week.

My arrival in Felixstowe was a bit of a shock. The town bore no resemblance to the colourful pages of the brochure I had been studying. It was, at least, very clean with a good assortment of neat and tidy shops. My room on the top floor had a lovely sea view and was very well furnished.

Nerves had rarely been a problem for me on stage, but my first encounter with the legendary Handel Evans had me very much on tenterhooks. I had never set foot in an orchestra pit before, nor played my drums before an audience.

Chapter 4

Handel was waiting for me in the theatre restaurant at the front of the Pavilion. He was a thin, smiling man in his sixties with an obvious toupée.

"It's Lumley!" he shouted out in the restaurant in a delightful Welsh accent. It seemed he had been a *Whacko!* fan. "I'm Handel. Welcome to the theatre!"

We chatted, and he gave me some sound advice. "Always watch me John, and only me - take no notice of anyone else. We must rely totally on each other."

The orchestra pit was enormous; you could have got the entire London Philharmonic into it. Handel marked out our space and explained where he wanted to place me, with good sight lines and as close to him as possible so he could direct, conduct and talk to me. He was impressed with my kit.

I stepped into the pit the next morning at 9.15 sharp as instructed. Handel was already making his preparations.

"May we have the music please!" he said. This was the moment I had been dreading. All Handel's parts were meticulously bound in leather folders, beautifully arranged and marked. Mine were in a scruffy cardboard file. They looked like the work of a colony of spiders which had been overdosing on tea, coffee and lager.

"Do the best you can with what you've been given" he said. "I'll re-write them for you when we know what's wanted."

I had never accompanied an organist before. Handel's playing was so clear that it sounded like all the instruments of an orchestra worked into one. He was an obvious master of his craft - unlike his percussionist.

I trod very carefully, not contributing any beats that weren't necessary. All went swimmingly well and I was getting well into it, until the magicians came on. Pat Hatton and Peggy were a highly-accomplished act who seemed to have travelled most of the world.

"I would like the drummer to keep his eye on ME the whole time during our performance" said Pat.

"He can't do both" said Handel. "Read the parts or keep his eye on you, which do you want?"

"I have suffered many times from out-of-time accompaniment. It is far better, if, he know what he is doing, for him to keep his eye on me" replied Pat. "We must be in perfect unison for the tricks to work."

No responsibility here, I thought.

Pat Hatton produced an Ali Baba basket from the wings and his wife Peggy clambered into it in her Marks & Spencer twin set. Then he produced twelve long swords.

"As I plunge each sword into the basket I want a drum roll as they go in and a cymbal crash when they reach their destination and bring a gasp from the audience! Do you understand?"

"Yes" I lied.

"I will then ask Peggy to wriggle in the basket!" We waited as she obliged. "Then I will drive eleven swords into it!"

"No you don't!" came an anguished cry from the basket. "I've got my top snagged!"

Handel saw the opportunity of a coup here.

"Is that part of the act?" he asked with a straight face. Pat glared at him.

The two comics, Jay Martel and Barry Johns, came on and rehearsed their sketches. They didn't seem very funny to me, but Handel explained they were working to a seaside audience and that I would be surprised on the night. Then the tenor and the soprano did their spot - thankfully they didn't need my services.

The show opened with a landladies' night, which went well. All the ladies were supposed to report back to their guests that this show must be the highlight of their week's holiday. They must have complied, as we were nearly always full.

My favourite number in the show was '*Little Drummer Boy*' which I soloed with the girl dancers. The girls challenged me by doing very fast tap breaks, which I had to follow. Some nights the girls would change their breaks to catch me out, but at the end of the season I think we were quits. It was great fun, and the 26 weeks flew by.

It was during my Felixstowe season that I found my first girlfriend. Aileen was cheerful and chirpy and a real joy to be with. We were good friends and mates, but to Megs' relief I never tried to smuggle her up to my room. I did treat her to dinner at the hotel on the last night of the show at the hotel. I returned home from my summer season to spend a quiet, lonely and rather pensive fortnight at home.

My acting career was not quite over yet. For the previous three years the BBC Drama Repertory Company had cast me in a children's adventure series called '*Charter Pilot*', in which Patricia Hayes played all the ground staff and I played the pilot's son, and very often a stowaway as well.

The BBC had put us all on a run-of-show contract, which meant they could call us back to do another 16 episodes whenever they wanted to. Although I was no longer looking for acting roles, I did enjoy this job, especially as the cast had become like a family over the years. The recordings were done in the same Birmingham studio where the Archers was made.

Going to Brum was a double treat for me as it meant staying with my adorable Auntie Millie. Aunt Millie was an inch over four feet tall, very

Chapter 4

Jewish and very proud. She was the most generous and loving of all my relatives. She bore the scars of the war with great dignity.

The BBC always sent Aunt Millie my scripts so that I could look through them on the Friday evening before rehearsals the following day. She was very proud to be entrusted by the BBC with such a valuable item, but the truth was that the writers very rarely finished the episodes in time to get them to us in London, so it was safer to drop them off where I was staying.

Aunt Millie would mark the pages where I had lines and underline my part. She would also add her own comments in the margins.

Aunt Millie and Uncle Lesley had a two-up, two-down house in the suburb of Acocks Green. Uncle Lesley would spend all day and evening chain smoking in his armchair facing the garden.

"He's had a hard war" she would say. I thought this rather ironic, as poor Millie had lost all her family and most of her friends to Hitler's concentration camps.

Each Saturday morning Millie would accompany me back to Acocks Green station and on to the train to Birmingham city centre, and we would walk together to the studios. Millie would see me right to the door of the studios and hand me my lunch, however much I tried to explain to her that we always had lunch in the canteen. She would also leave me at the door, however much I pleaded with her to come inside and meet the actors and put faces to the voices, as I knew she would dearly love to do.

It wasn't long before I had a chance to put this right. We would always hold a farewell party after the last episode. Most of the cast of *The Archers* had guested for us in one or another of the episodes, so that year we decided we would celebrate with them at an Italian restaurant which was handily situated between the studio and Broad Street Station.

Chapter 4

Millie and I had to pass the restaurant on our way to the station. On the night of the party I made sure I let the others go on first to the restaurant. As we passed it, I turned to Millie.

"I need to go to the toilet" I said.

"Surely you can wait till we get to the station?"

"No I can't - I need to go now. Don't worry, they know me in here. You can just wait inside for me. I'll only be a couple of minutes."

"OK" she added anxiously, "Don't be any longer!" We stepped inside and I slipped away into the restaurant.

"May I take your coat, Madame?" Auntie Millie was suddenly confronted by the head waiter with a sherry on a tray for her.

"No, no. I'm just waiting for my nephew - he won't be a minute."

"I believe he has gone to Ambridge, Madam" said the waiter.

"I beg your pardon? He's gone to the toilet!!"

The waiter took her arm and drew her into the restaurant.

"May I introduce you to Walter Gabriel?" he said, and out came the actor Chris Gittins, who played the role. Aunt Millie nearly collapsed when 'Walter' gave her a kiss on the cheek. And then a massive cheer went up from the restaurant as over 30 actors and actresses sang a chorus of 'For she's a jolly good fellow'.

Auntie Millie couldn't speak after that, let alone walk to the station. I had to treat us to a taxi.

Charter Pilot came to an abrupt end two years later, when Robert Marsden died suddenly of a heart attack. Eleven weeks later, the same thing

Chapter 4

happened to dear Auntie Millie. How lucky I was to have had all that love and affection. Love's last gift is always remembrance.

Chapter 5

They brought me sunshine

There was nothing acrimonious about my parents' separation and eventual divorce. They always showed a huge respect and love for each other. My mother's beauty, my father's courage; a perfect match.

Two problems did for their marriage; the lack of time my mother could spend at home, and my father's inability to accept her fame.

At the divorce hearing, the magistrate gave custody of me to my father because my mother was away so much. She was very upset about this, but she needn't have worried - within the hour my father had handed me back. He wanted to live footloose and free in Paris, and having a child on his hands was the last thing he wanted.

Far from resenting it, I shall forever be in my father's debt for his decision, for I went on to have the most wonderful childhood in the care of two wonderful women.

Like my father's parents, my parents decided to create a touring company - a venture which proved much more successful and enduring than their marriage. The French Theatre Company or La Troupe Française consisted entirely of French actors studying and working in the UK. The idea was to benefit students studying French for their exams, so my parents would be careful to choose plays which were on that year's syllabus such as *Le Barbier de Séville*, *Le Malade Imaginaire* and *Cyrano de Bergerac*.

Chapter 5

The Troupe became hugely successful. It lasted 35 years. My parents were both well qualified to play the leading roles (my mother had performed in France with the Comédie Française). The *'Barber'* was my father's favourite, because it gave him the opportunity to throw in some of his splendid singing. This always brought the house down, as it was so unexpected.

Each year my parents signed up six to eight French actors and actresses. These young players would be eager to join the Troupe for a three-month tour, because they knew they'd be staying in top hotels and eating good food. They would arrive in a city like Manchester and take over the Palace for a week, giving two performances a day to 4000 school children plus their teachers.

Many of the performances were given at public schools like Harrow, Rugby, Eton and Roedean, but because both my parents were keen to see that as many people as possible should benefit from seeing the production, around half the shows were put on in towns and villages around Britain where there was little opportunity to see such productions. As a result the Troupe played in gymnasiums, assembly halls, canteens - even classrooms and playgrounds.

This idea of taking theatre out to ordinary people in ordinary places was very much ahead of its time. It must have been quite an experience to rise at seven on a freezing winter's day and perform a three-hour French classic to an audience of schoolchildren in Merthyr Tydfil.

My parents were keen to involve me in their venture. I was bilingual, so performing in French would be no problem. It would save them money - and from my point of view it would give me a rare chance to be with both my parents at once.

It became harder when they alternated the tours. My mother would lead one company with Claude, my stepfather-to-be, while my father's company would always include Odile, my stepmother-to-be. I was constantly having to walk on eggshells to avoid upsetting one camp or the other. But when they worked together, Mum and Dad were dynamite. Their comedy routines and their timing made them wonderful to watch.

During my first tour with La Troupe Française I played all the minor parts that helped to make the cast look more impressive at the curtain call. I was usually costumed in thigh-length boots, very often with an oversized sword dangling from my belt, a plumed hat and, of course, coloured tights. Not the most comfortable attire, especially as we had to wear a box instead of the normal zip. When we played to the girls' colleges I had to endure the mirth and ridicule of a horde of laughing girls. It made me all the more determined to carry out my promise to myself to give up acting.

When we presented *Cyrano de Bergerac,* my father suggested I bring along my drum kit for the tour so that I could contribute some atmospheric 'noises off' to the play's battle scene. This did not really come off as there were only three actors in the scene. However, the drums were a big hit with George, our helpful and friendly driver, with whom I had struck up a friendship. I agreed to give him lessons.

At the end of the twelve weeks we had all lost our voices and the French actors were dying to get back home across the Channel. It was my one-and-only tour with my parents, and I never even got to drive the van.

>-I-+>-O-<+I-<>-I-+>-O-<+I-<

During our visit with the Troupe to the Palace Theatre in Manchester, I had demonstrated some proficiency in setting up the stage, running the prompt corner, managing the lighting cues and such matters. In the early

Chapter 5

1960s I was approached by the two resident stage managers, Bert and Jeff, along with the electrician, Gill Binks. They asked me if I would consider stage-managing that season's pantomime, *Sleeping Beauty*.

This was a very lavish Tom Arnold production which was coming to Manchester directly from the London Palladium, where it had broken all box office records. The stars were Morecambe and Wise, who were already firmly at the top of the light entertainment tree.

I was surprised, flattered, and a little frightened. I hadn't trained in stage management and wasn't at all sure I was up to such a responsibility. And after all I was still only nineteen years old. But I well understood that the entertainment industry is all about seizing opportunities, and I would be a fool not to seize this one.

Bert and Jeff sent me to London to meet Tom Arnold's production manager, Lawrence Green. Green was a tall, elegant man in his sixties, quietly spoken but authoritative. I remember being mesmerised by the perfection of the Windsor knot in his tie. Ever since that meeting I have tried unsuccessfully to emulate that knot.

I was offered tea next door, at Simpson's of Piccadilly.

"You come highly recommended, Mr Stirling" said Mr Green. "You will find the size of the production rather daunting at first. Morecambe and Wise are the hottest property this country has, and they have to be looked after with kid gloves. However, they are both charming and very easy to get on with - as long as everything is right! Do you understand?"

"Yes sir" I quaked.

"They have served long and arduous apprenticeships to get to where they are, and now that their requirements are somewhat more demanding you will need to be there to look after them."

Chapter 5

"I'll do my best" I quavered.

"No-one can ask for more, Mr Stirling! You will start in Manchester first week in December and the show will close on April 26th. The scenery lorries arrive first, so I want you to go down to our stores near Brighton and acquaint yourself with the sets. The brothers down there are helpful and will construct them for you so you'll know how to erect them when they arrive in Manchester.

"You will also be required to understudy Ernie Wise in his part as the jester. With your background, that shouldn't be a problem."

I stared in disbelief.

He saw my expression of panic. "It's just a formality" he assured me. "If Eric or Ernie can't perform, neither of them will. But you will run the understudy calls, and it helps everyone if you stand in too."

I signed the contract with trembling fingers, before I could change my mind.

My first call (after a celebratory tea with my mother, of course) was to Aileen, my girlfriend from Felixstowe. We had stayed in constant touch, and I was missing her. I told her to keep buying *The Stage* each week until she saw the advertisement for dancers for the production.

"I'll never get into that show" she said.

"I did" I replied.

"Bloody hell!" she said.

The day arrived and Aileen travelled down for the auditions. Fortunately I had been asked to attend, in my position as stage manager. Aileen was looking very anxious, as 400 girls had turned up to audition for twelve places. But she had lost weight and was looking wonderful.

Chapter 5

After six hours of gruelling work, Irving Davies, the choreographer, whittled the 400 down to twelve. Aileen was one of them. I was nearly as pleased as she was - I wouldn't have to be alone for all those weeks in Manchester.

We rented a flat in Moss Side and invited six other dancers, four girls and two boys, to share it with us to keep the rent down - the show might have been big, but our wages were modest. We each had our own room and shared a kitchen and bathroom.

The lorries with the scenery arrived, and with them a huge responsibility. I was the only person who knew where everything went and how it was all constructed. I allowed Bert and Jeff the space to do it their way first, but when they got into trouble, I stepped in and put everything back in its place, without any fuss. This got the stagehands on my side and earned the respect of Bert and Jeff.

It took two and a half days to get the revolving stage in place and revolving correctly. None of us saw our beds for two nights.

During the first week Irving Davies and his dancers had the stage to themselves. Aileen did well and was given lots of little cameos. Irving even chose her to do a minuet with Eric Morecambe.

In the second week the principals started to arrive. Edmund Hockridge, the Prince, was very affable and ruggedly good-looking - every inch the musical star. He had just had a massive hit in *Pyjama Game* at the London Coliseum and his song *Hey there, you with the stars in your eyes* was in the charts.

Eddie Malloy, who played the Dame, was rotund, bubbly and amiable. After he had been spotted by Morecambe and Wise, the duo insisted on his playing the role whenever they appeared in *Sleeping Beauty*. Eric found him the perfect foil.

Chapter 5

I have never thought of myself as the starstruck type, but the day Morecambe and Wise arrived I couldn't stop myself grinning like a teenage girl. When Eric walked on to the stage for the first time, the place erupted. Irving had to break off rehearsals so that the dancers could go over and say hello to the pair.

Eric was charming, funny, and very considerate. He made a point of going over to everyone associated with the production and chatting to them all as if he had known them for years. Ernie was charming too, but he was clearly the business half of the partnership.

When the pair met on stage it was magic. There was a superb chemistry between them. They had an extraordinary way of reacting spontaneously to each other, and their timing was phenomenal. Each seemed to know what the other was going to do before he did it. They made it all look so easy.

The way the pair handled the press and television was a lesson to us all. They were a magnificent public relations team who made sure everyone knew when the show was going to open and when it would finish.

I had arranged their dressing rooms as they had requested. They never shared, because they felt that if they met up on stage the encounter would be that much fresher. Eric's room was on the prompt side of the stage and at the same level, so he had only to walk out of his room to be on stage. He decorated his room with photos of his wife, children and friends to make his dressing room a home-from-home - Joan was back home, as their children were still at school.

Ernie's room was on the OP (opposite prompt) side. He shared his room with his wife Doreen, who was also his assistant, along with their Scots terrier. Both men had lounges where they could rest or entertain friends. TV and phone lines had been installed, but neither Eric nor Ernie ever used them - they preferred privacy.

Chapter 5

I have never witnessed a first night like it. Never can an audience have responded with such love and affection as they did to these two men. Happiness reigned from the moment the curtain went up until the house lights came on at the end. Even now, after all my years in this business, I can't remember seeing anything or anyone get the response Morecambe and Wise achieved that night.

Eric certainly needed looking after, as Lawrence Green had predicted. He didn't seem to be able to go anywhere or do anything for himself. He was just about the most famous man in England, yet his loneliness was all too apparent.

I had to be there to see people into his dressing room, but more importantly to see them out again. Eric couldn't finish anything. It was much easier for someone else to make the excuses for him. Time was precious to him - he had very little of it to himself and he would tire quickly with his relentless schedule. In addition to performing in the panto twice a day, the pair were expected to rehearse for their forthcoming TV series, edit their first feature film, even open shops. It must have been intensely gruelling.

It was difficult to go anywhere with Eric, because he was always recognised with or without his glasses. And without them he couldn't see where he was going anyway. I would get his meals and Eddie Malloy would deal with his bets at Gus Demmy's, the bookmaker next door to the theatre. Eric would ask Eddie on stage during the performance if his horse had won. Once Eddie paid Eric his winnings on stage, which took Eric by surprise and got a big laugh. It wasn't often anyone got one over on Eric.

But I could see why he liked working with Eddie Malloy - he would send him up mercilessly. "Have you shaved your legs?" he would ask, or "What about that hair under your nose?" Eddie knew which side his bread was buttered and kept up his part as if nothing had happened.

Chapter 5

Sleeping Beauty was a mammoth hit. Eric and Ernie's film *The Magnificent Two* was showing at The Odeon Cinema next door, so the whole of Oxford Road was lit up by Britain's top comedy duo.

Eric greatly appreciated all the trouble we took on his behalf and he in turn he would try to help those around him. He was intrigued that I had given up a successful acting career and liked to listen to my stories about my adventures in radio and on the stage. He even tried to encourage my love of light entertainment by suggesting to Lesley Grade that he should use me in their forthcoming summer shows.

I remember just one crisis from that run of *Sleeping Beauty* - one I still have nightmares about forty-odd years later. One Monday morning, the company manager and I were summoned to the Midland Hotel across the road from the theatre. When we arrived, we were met in reception by Doreen Wise. She was looking very worried.

"Ernie has swallowed his bottom teeth" she said. "The plate has got jammed in his throat. They have taken him to Manchester Royal Infirmary, but they've told me he won't be back today as they are still not sure how to get it out. So he won't be able to do today's shows."

The manager and I looked at each other in horror. As we left the foyer, the lift doors opened to reveal Eric. He beckoned us up to his penthouse suite on the sixth floor.

"Sit down and have a coffee" he said. "Look, there is an agreement I have to honour and I have no intention of breaking it. If one of us is not able to appear, we both stand down.

"I've talked to Doreen and she has agreed that we should let the show go ahead with the understudies. I'll come on and explain the problem so that the audience doesn't feel totally cheated. John will play the jester and the boy dancer will play the King. Eddie will fall in all the holes. I'll appear at both shows and have an informal chat with the audience. It'll work, don't worry, they will understand. And you won't have to give everybody their money back."

With much trepidation, we agreed to Eric's plan. I had attended the understudy rehearsals in a supervisory capacity only, as it had been made clear that my services would never be required. Yet here I was having to play the lead, opposite a boy dancer who was equally terrified.

As it happened, both performances went quite well, thanks to Eric's brief appearances. In the second show, during a scene in the royal court when everybody was supposed to be in a deep sleep, I nodded off for real. The cast couldn't keep a straight face as Eric crept on to the stage and awoke me with a kiss so that the scene could carry on.

I will never forget the curtain call. Eric made me come down last. He stepped forward and told the audience that Ernie had recovered, which got a standing ovation. Then he turned to me, slapped me on both cheeks, and down came the curtain.

"I must apologise for John, who was very average in place of Ernie" he said. "He was quite honestly dreadful. It made Ernie very happy, so he had to open his purse and give the lad some coppers he had.

"I want to say that from Eddie's hairy legs to the fat dancer, the fairies, the goblins, the princes, the princess and Gus Demmy next door, who found the whole experience very harrowing, that we all love the boy very much and one day I'll let him do his blackbird impression. That's all for now." He clapped and the company joined in. I was truly embarrassed, but delighted. There are some moments in one's life which we know we'll remember forever, and that was one of them.

Chapter 5

To our great relief, Ernie was back on stage as normal the following day. Eric never let him forget the day he had swallowed his teeth, and he had to endure weeks of jokes about dentistry and root canal work. And he insisted that he was not to be smacked on the cheeks for a fortnight.

That night Aileen took me out to dinner in the city centre. Over the meal she leaned over the table and looked into my eyes. I braced myself. "When he said the fat dancer - did he mean me?" she asked. "Of course not!" I smiled back.

Chapter 6

Situations vacant

Eric Morecambe's influence with Lesley Grade had borne fruit. I was given a new assignment for the summer of 1966 - a season as stage director at the Britannia Pier in Great Yarmouth, in a Bernard Delfont show starring Bob Monkhouse. That, however, was still some weeks away, and I had to find something to do in the meantime which would keep the wolf from the door.

When *Sleeping Beauty* finished, it was down to earth for all of us for a while. Aileen went back to Kettering and to stacking shelves in Woolworths. Such are the ups and downs of show business. I returned to the classified pages of *The Stage*, and it wasn't long before an advertisement caught my attention.

'To All Resting Actors! Call Domestics Unlimited now to fill that gap between jobs. We guarantee your anonymity and excellent hourly rates!' it read.

The offices were in Wardour Street in the West End, which sounded reassuringly upmarket. The reality was a little different. I climbed four flights of wooden stairs to a tiny room which looked as if it had been used to store the mops and buckets.

There was a single desk with a telephone. The elderly lady sitting there looked as if she had spent longer on her makeup than a professional drag queen - there were at least three layers of foundation, several pounds of

Chapter 6

blue eye-shadow and thick lines of mascara. The lipstick looked as if it had been put on with a spade. Her false nails were so long that when she typed it sounded like a construction site in full flow.

"How long have you been out of work, dearie?' she asked me.

"Four days" I replied, wondering what on earth I was doing there.

"Anything in the pipeline?"

"Yes - I'm going to Great Yarmouth for a summer season."

"That's nice, dearie. So you're just looking for temporary work for a month or so. Is that right, dearie?"

"Definitely."

"We clean people's houses, from top to bottom. We use actors because they have been very successful for us in the past. They show a great talent for it." She giggled, which didn't help to put me at my ease.

"I see" I replied, reflecting that to date I had never even cleaned my own bedroom.

"It's very hard work, but well paid. It's a whole day from nine to five and they are normally big houses with demanding clients, who want blood!" She wasn't doing a great job of selling this job to me. But I needed the money.

"OK, I'll give it a go" I said.

"That's the spirit." My new employer opened a drawer of her filing cabinet, extended two of the nails of her right hand like the prongs of a forklift truck, and hoisted out a contract.

"I'm going to send you to a big house in Richmond for your first job" she said. "It's one of our regulars."

Chapter 6

"May I ask who it is?"

"You may not" she said severely. "We never divulge our client base. You'll find out soon enough. Be there at 9 am sharp. Mrs Bridges the housekeeper will be expecting you."

When I got home, my grandmother was highly amused at my new 'role'. "You, a domestic - certainly not typecasting this time" she laughed. "You don't even know how to put on a pair of rubber gloves!"

Richmond was a short ride from Putney on the no. 30 bus. The house I had been directed to was a beautiful mansion in its own grounds, enclosed by black and gold railings with a huge double-gated entrance. I walked down the path, admiring the gardens, the pond, the water features and the two cars in the double garage. I spotted a sign to the service entrance and followed it to the back of the house.

A lady in full domestic uniform, complete with mob cap, opened the door – the real Mrs Bridges.

"I do hope you're not going to waste my time like the last one they sent" she said. She led me down to the basement and into an enormous kitchen. "We have a ten-minute break for tea at eleven and fifteen minutes at one o'clock" she said. "Have you brought sandwiches?" I hadn't. "Never mind, at least it'll be a chance to sit down. You'll remember next time."

"Our last break is for tea at four and you'll be done by five. Your mops, buckets, floorcloths, washing-up liquid, floor polish, bath enamel cream, Brillo pads, dusters and rubber gloves are in that cupboard. Start at the top of the house and work your way down. All the toilets to be done thoroughly, floors scrubbed, you leave only the beds - I do those. Understood?" I nodded, wondering if I should have been writing it all down.

As I reached the first landing, a man came out of the bathroom in a dressing-gown, towelling his face. "Hello" he said kindly. "Have you come to do for us?" I knew his face from somewhere, but I couldn't think where.

"Good luck!" he said, disappearing into a room across the landing. And then I realised who it was - Bryan Forbes, the actor and film director.

I climbed to the next landing, where an elegant lady was sitting at a desk, writing. I recognised her from the Dickens series I'd done. It was Nanette Newman.

"Hello John!" she said. "What on earth are you doing here?"

"Starting at the top" I said and disappeared quickly up to the next landing.

Five minutes later, as I was cleaning the loo on my hands and knees, Bryan joined me again.

"Wasn't your father in *The Cruel Sea*?"

"Yes" I said in a muffled voice, getting deeper and deeper into the loo. The embarrassment was hard to take.

"What will Pamela think of us, letting you clean our toilet?" he reflected. "I'm just going to have a word with the housekeeper."

"Oh hell" I thought. "Fired before I start."

Mrs Bridges was ordered to make tea for me, which rather put her nose out of joint. Bryan and Nanette told me to give my mother their very best, and sent me on my way.

The next day I got a phone call from the agency.

"Hello dearie, sorry about yesterday" she said. "Never mind, I've got you down for Patricia Hayes in East Putney today."

"I don't think so" I said and put the phone down. A lucky escape.

Chapter 6

Goodness knows what Pat would have said if I'd turned up on her doorstep with a mop and bucket.

In the extended family of the theatrical world, word soon gets out if any of its members fall by the wayside. The jungle telegraph began to beat overtime with messages of sympathy to my mother and concern that she had had to send her one and only son to the workhouse. This was unfair, as it had been entirely my own decision to apply to Domestics Unlimited.

It all came to a head a week later when Margaret Rawlings, a great friend of the family, rang up. Margaret had been a very respected star of film and theatre. Having married Lord Barlow of the Metal Box Company, she was now Lady Barlow.

Margaret was distraught. The story had become distorted on its way around the grapevine, and she seemed to be under the impression that I had been reduced to cleaning out the toilets at Brompton Oratory. She started giving both my mother and my grandmother a piece of her mind for allowing the family name to reach such depths.

My mother managed to set the record straight, and eventually Lady Barlow was pacified.

"I must do something, just to make life a little easier for him" she said.

"That boy needs for nothing" said my mother. It was a line straight out of Charles Dickens.

"Nonsense" came the reply. "I must do something, and indeed I have thought of something which I hope he will be able to accept." My mother listened attentively.

"Several actor friends of mine take up mini-cab driving when they are resting. If I could get him a car, that would give him a second string to his bow, wouldn't it?"

"It seems an awful lot" said my mother.

"That's for me to decide. Ask him if the idea would appeal to him, and then get him to ring me."

It wasn't exactly a hard decision to make, and I didn't have to wrestle with it for long. A new car of my own!

The car arrived about ten days later. I had imagined something modest and basic such as a Mini, but I had underestimated my benefactor. There before me, parked outside my house, was a brand new top-of-the-range Mark 2 Ford Cortina in Titanium Silver.

The man from the garage presented me with the keys and explained where everything was. The car was fully taxed and ready to go. I sat in it for the rest of the morning, marvelling at the new-car smell, the clock, the cigarette lighter, the sunshades, the wood veneer dash, the folding armrests and the radio (quite a luxury back then).

Unfortunately, sit was all I could do. I hadn't dared tell Lady Barlow that I hadn't yet learned to drive.

Fortunately I remembered George, the driver I had made friends with while touring with La Troupe Française. When I told him what had happened, he came to the rescue without hesitating. Ten weeks later, under George's guidance, I was able to pass my driving test.

That gift from Lady Barlow changed my life. I no longer had to ask for lifts. I could take my parents wherever they wanted to go.

I couldn't imagine how I would ever be able to thank her properly, but it wasn't long before an opportunity presented itself. At the time she was appearing at the Mayfair Theatre in the West End in her one-woman show, *The Princess Eugénie*. This was quite a journey for her each day backwards and forwards from her home in Dorking, and she had been relying on a hired car and chauffeur. I offered to pick her up each day, take her to the theatre, collect her after the show and take her home, if necessary taking her friends home too at the end of the evening. She was delighted.

I never did get to do any mini-cabbing. By the time I had passed my test and finished my chauffeuring for Lady Barlow, it was time to head off to Great Yarmouth for the start of my first season as a stage director.

Even in early May, Great Yarmouth was a busy place. It had five theatres, a circus, a bowling alley, a ballroom, a fun fair, a bandstand, a cricket ground, a miniature golf course and a football pitch - all a far cry from little old Felixstowe.

The promenade was flanked at each end by a pier, each with a theatre at its end. I would be working on the Britannia Pier, while the theatre on the Wellington Pier was presenting a show with Bruce Forsyth and Matt Monroe. In between the piers was the Windmill Theatre, where Tommy Steele and Frankie Howerd were starring, while at the ABC Cliff Richard was playing with the Shadows. I was in opulent company. Eric and Ernie had always said how much they enjoyed their seasons here, and I could see why.

The stars went to great lengths to encourage and promote their support acts, and I learned an important lesson - that when the star at the top of the bill is happy, the whole company benefits.

In the middle of the high street was the Savoy restaurant. The Savoy would close its upstairs off to the general public at 10.30 each night and reopen for the artists; twelve tables of ten were taken up every night in the season. The prices were low enough for everyone in the company to take advantage of these sessions. The stars could enjoy themselves undisturbed by rubberneckers from the general public.

Chapter 6

These evenings were great fun. Very often one of the performers would give an impromptu cabaret. Tommy would play guitar, Bruce would dance, Bob would crack a few jokes or Matt Monroe would give us that wonderful voice, all into the early hours.

Stage direction was all very well, but I desperately wanted to be part of all this. Eric and Ernie had given me a taste for the limelight which I couldn't shake off.

At the end of the season, there was a midnight matinée. All the theatres and their companies congregated in the Britannia Pier Theatre and put on a variety show to top all variety shows. It ran from midnight to three in the morning and raised many thousands of pounds for Brinsworth House, a residential care home for artists who had no means of looking after themselves in their twilight years.

Bob Monkhouse was shy and quite reserved off stage, and suffered from nerves. He didn't make life easier for himself by insisting on topical material, which meant he had to write his act from the daily newspapers shortly before the performance. It was clever stuff, but immensely time consuming. But Bob was extraordinarily skilled with words, as I was to find out later to my advantage.

I particularly enjoyed the Morton Fraser Harmonica Gang with the Midget. I also liked Jill Day, who supported Bob with her singing, but my favourite act of all was the Witchwoods, a young couple with 23 miniature white poodles. The dogs rode bikes, walked tightropes, rolled in barrels and during the twelve-minute act would strip all the clothing off their masters, leaving them to take a bow in their underclothes. The finale was the House of Cards, where all 23 dogs were placed in a castle of cards which then collapsed with no sign of the dogs anywhere - quite brilliant.

September and the end of the summer season came all too soon.

Chapter 6

The holidaymakers trickled away and Great Yarmouth began to go into hibernation for the winter. Ours was the last show to finish, so by the time the curtain went down for the last time the town was pretty much deserted.

Actors have to learn to say goodbye. It was very strange to have to return home to the domestic routine of Putney after six months of non-stop parties, dinners and camaraderie, to say nothing of putting on two shows a night.

For the resting actor there is always a period of readjustment, of reconnection with the outside world. A mild depression sets in, a condition which can only be cured by the advent of another job, the opening of new doors and encounters with new friends and colleagues.

My return was strange for my family, too. I became uncomfortably aware that they had rather enjoyed the freedom I had given them through my six-month absence.

My mother and Claude had taken to spending their evenings upstairs in his study. Mum was starring in a long-running French soap called *Bonjour Françoise* and Claude was working overtime with his daily programme, *Bâton Rompu*. My grandmother was needed to look after my young sister Marie-Victoire, who was now not only very beautiful but showing all the academic prowess that I had lacked.

Nookie and I spent most of our spare time together in her room among a labyrinth of bookshelves stacked to the ceiling like a reference library on the theatre. Her photos and portraits of friends like George Bernard Shaw adorned the wall over her bed. We would sit by the fire reminiscing about her theatre days and of the many times she had chaperoned me.

Much as I was made welcome back home, there was one rather obvious hint that my mother and Claude were hoping I would not be staying with them for too long this time. They had left beside my bed a large advertisement from *The Stage*. It seemed that the British telephone service was recruiting out-of-work, French-speaking actors and actresses to join their international operator service at the exchange at Blackfriars. Men were expected to join the night shift.

Ideally I would have liked a little time to find something more in line with my true interests, but I knew my parents and Nookie would not be happy if I lingered at home too long. I duly applied for the job.

On the day of the interview I turned up at Faraday House, Blackfriars Bridge on the Embankment promptly at two. The building was as grey and dull as the autumn day, a cold, tiled, cavernous place which had been built as a hospital. It made me think of Dotheboys Hall in *Nicholas Nickleby*. The walls were tiled in white from floor to ceiling. I felt as if I was going to authenticate a body in a mortuary.

I made my way along a corridor to find a long wooden bench where thirty or forty people sat waiting to be summoned. A stern-looking man with a clipboard appeared. "Jean-Pierre Richer?" he enquired. It had been my grandmother's idea to use my French name for this job, partly for anonymity in the theatre world and partly because she thought they would be impressed by the French name.

I went into the interview room to find four people sitting behind an old wooden refectory table. Behind the panel of judges, a grimy full-length window with broken blinds allowed what little sunlight there was to be directed straight into my face.

The lady who started the grilling was French, which gave me a chance to demonstrate my ability in the language, and we had a friendly chat. The next questioner didn't seem to like this much. It seemed he was an Elocution and Enunciation Officer. Well, that wasn't too bad; after all I had been to drama school. The third member was from the telephone company, and all he could talk about was phone technology. The last person was the personnel officer. He made the telephone boffin seem interesting by comparison.

My references went down well, although the personnel manager couldn't resist attempting an impression of Eric Morecambe, which was received with blank amazement by his fellow members. It served to remind us all why some people are professional comics and some, frankly, should stick to their day jobs.

Finally, they all faced front. "The most important factor here is your obvious qualification in the language stakes" said the leader. "What we have to decide is whether you would be willing and able to complete the eighteen weeks' training, as many fall by the wayside and the training is very thorough and expensive. A class of thirty usually finishes up with three operators, if we're lucky."

He went on to explain that I would have to sign the Official Secrets Act. Then he told me I would be handed over to the personnel manager. I had got the job.

I wondered how I was going to explain to this rather staid man that my insurance card and tax codes were in the name of John Stirling. It took three hours for the paperwork to be sorted out.

I was told to report to Faraday House for training the following Monday. They issued me with a badge. I smiled and asked if there was a similar pass to get out, which was met with stony silence. It was clear that any attempt at levity was not going to be welcomed.

I was given information about the union I would have to join and issued with three heavy manuals to study and a 74-page encyclopaedia on the intricacies of wiring and cabling across Europe. Finally there was a technical guide to the switchboard I would be operating. Lots and lots of reading - just my cup of tea.

The news that only four people had been offered the eighteen-week induction - and that I was the only one who had accepted it - sent me into a deep depression. This was worse than school - it was Dotheboys Hall indeed.

The work was as tedious as I had feared. Hour after hour of sticking in your plug, taking it out again, dialling codes, handling breakdown calls, rerouting. Most of the callers spoke in unintelligible accents and seemed to feel they had the right to abuse the operators freely.

One night I was able to report to my grandmother that I had had to put Harold Wilson, the Prime Minister, through to Brussels - he was charming and spoke perfect French. She loathed Mr Wilson, and sulked for days at this news.

After three months we were introduced to the main international switchboard, which had 20 positions on one massive board. The board was so tall that we had to stand on our stools to reach the top. Wires were hanging from everywhere. When you saw a red light come up your heart just stopped.

To learn the ropes I sat next to an experienced operator on a night shift. I couldn't believe what I saw. The wires looked like an accident in a knitting shop. Yet he obviously knew exactly where each one was connected. He must have been taking fifteen calls a minute, writing the numbers on his dockets for reference, all the time talking politely to someone down the line. I was impressed, and horrified.

I got on well with this chap - it turned out that by day he was one of the senior designers at the Old Vic. He was doing the nights to make ends meet. He said it also helped his drink problem.

"Just think of it as spare cash John, then you'll get through it" he advised me. "Sooner or later it all falls into place."

Astonishingly, I managed to finish my training and work on the exchange. I could see why we had had to sign the Official Secrets Act, as I dealt with many top politicians on both sides of the channel. But my favourite will always be Elizabeth Taylor. She was sweet and patient, despite the length of time she had to wait for her connections each night.

And then life took another turn, in the shape of a phone call with my name on it. The caller was Bob Monkhouse. Bob explained to me that he had become involved in a showbiz venture of a different kind, and he had a job for me.

I can't begin to explain how wonderful it felt when Bob saved me from the spaghetti nightmare of that telephone exchange and brought me back to the life I knew and loved. Pulling out my plug for the last time was a moment I still savour.

I walked from 'Dotheboys Hall' straight into the gleaming world of the West End. Here in Park Lane were the sumptuous offices of Mitchell Monkhouse Associates, whose directors were Bob, Alan Mitchell and Denis Goodman. Bob and Denis were already famous for their comedy-writing partnership, but they were now leaning towards corporate entertainment. MMA helped the captains of industry to put on conferences and promotional events. They staged, styled and wrote them, developing new corporate images and logos and gave expert media advice. They hired the best hotels, built ambitious sets, choreographed the event, created the menus and directed the whole proceedings, with devastating effect. The blue-chip companies were queueing up for this service and MMA's clients ranged from Coca Cola to Rank Xerox and from Hewlett

Chapter 6

Packard to Mars, Maxwell House and Players.

This was where business met show business. Huge sets travelled around the country. There were chorus lines, singers, actors and orchestras. Game shows were a favourite - Bob excelled in both creating and appearing in these, and if he wasn't free to front one himself there were always other stars available. We built a complete railway station with track and a train with two carriages; we constructed an island in the Bristol Rooms with a full size galleon bringing the pirates to plunder.

It was enormous fun transforming these huge function rooms and ballrooms for entertainment. My favourite was the time we recreated the front of Buckingham Palace, gravel, railings and all, then with a massive drum roll brought in the entire band of the Coldstream Guards. Wonderful stuff. The American and Japanese businessmen rose to their feet to show their appreciation. It all cost a fortune, but the client made their money back ten times over.

We would travel around the country with six pantechnicons, carrying crews of stage hands and roadies, carpenters and lighting engineers, sound crews and painters. There were motor shows, boat shows and horse shows. Each time we'd be given three days to perform miracles, and each time we pulled it off.

One night at The Dorchester Hotel, as part of conference for Coca Cola, we brought in pop stars. Bob introduced me to a young entrepreneur by the name of Larry Parnes. Larry was there to keep an eye on his protégé - Billy Fury, who was headlining the cabaret.

On stage Billy was a sex god; off it, he was painfully shy and retiring. Parnes had managed Billy very cleverly. He had turned this self-effacing one-time Mersey Ferry dockhand into a star.

He made sure Billy was never seen before going on stage, which suited

Billy fine. He would disguise him and devise intricate routes to enable to get in and out of venues in secret, because there is no doubt that if Billy ever got into the hands of those fans he would have been torn to shreds. Once Larry built a huge backcloth with a convincing brick wall pattern, then started the show by driving Billy's car through the wall on to the stage.

Just once Billy was caught outside the theatre, when we turned up at Blackpool in a Mini with black windows and the girls actually surrounded the car and bodily carried it down the road away from the stage door. Poor Billy stayed put inside until the Blackpool Fire Brigade transferred him from the Mini to a fire engine and took him safely back to the theatre.

Larry asked me to take care of Billy Fury during the conference. I found Billy a lovely man, though so reserved that he wasn't far removed from a hermit. He spoke in a very quick, gentle voice; everything he did was done with great serenity and calm. But on stage, he was electric. He would stand quietly in the wings waiting to go on, shy and peaceful, and then as soon as the spotlight shone he switched on the sex appeal and became a different man. His voice was not one of the greatest, but Larry chose his songs carefully and Billy had notched up a string of hits.

I have never come across any singer who was so commanding a performer on stage, and at the same time so marvellous a person to know in private. The fans never glimpsed Billy's extraordinary sensitivity and frailty when they weren't watching.

One thing which particularly endeared me to Billy was his love of animals - all animals. He would rescue everything from ants to foxes and hedgehogs to badgers, and he always took the latest protégés with him on tour. We would have an owl one week, a raccoon the next, a squirrel, even a monkey. He supported the animal charities anonymously, putting on concerts for them.

Chapter 6

Larry Parnes asked me to do a new summer show with Billy which was to be produced at The Royal Aquarium, Great Yarmouth. I was glad to accept as I loved the place and I was flattered to hear from Parnes that Billy had asked for me personally.

It was the first time Billy had attempted such a show on his own but Parnes had made quite sure the support and production were strong to support him. He brought in a new Australian entertainer called Rolf Harris, who had just had a hit with a song called *Tie Me Kangaroo Down Sport*, a new compère called Mike Yarwood and the Marty Wilde Trio. With a strong chorus of dancers and singers, two soubrettes, an orchestra in the pit and Billy's backing group, The Gamblers, it was a strong lineup.

Rolf Harris was a revelation. He worked with the dancers, brought on huge paintboards and made all the children in the audience scream with joy. He always came across as very lovable both on and off stage. And he could never sit still. In between working or rehearsing he would be designing pictures, doing portraits of the cast, even carving Christmas cards out of coconut matting. At the end of the season, he made extraordinary last-night gifts for everyone from different-shaped pebbles and shells he had collected from the Norfolk beaches. I still have mine.

The first thing Larry Parnes wanted me to do for Billy was find a hideaway where he could live quietly and privately for the sixteen weeks. Once I'd found one, Larry wanted to rehearse the different routes Billy could take to get to the theatre without being noticed. It helped that Billy liked to arrive very early, hours before the shows.

By the time we went into rehearsals we had worked out four escape routes and twelve arrival routes. One run went up a fire escape, across the theatre roof and down into the dressing room through an outside window. Billy was fond of that one!

Chapter 6

Billy's entrance on stage was of superstar proportions. He was beautifully turned out in a white jacket, dark trousers and satin shirt, with a quiff that fell over his forehead which he flicked back if there was a lull in the screaming. The girls were ten deep at the orchestra rails, screaming, tearing their clothes off, throwing roses - the whole works. His appearance kept the St John's Ambulance Brigade team on their toes for over an hour.

Billy had to be careful with his health as he had a heart condition, so we arranged his work schedules to allow rest periods. I find it so sad that thanks to his heart problems, brought on by rheumatic fever in childhood, Billy lived only another fifteen years; he died when he was just 43. I've worked with a lot of pop stars, but Billy was the finest of them all.

Each Sunday Larry Parnes would present a Sunday pop concert, and we were treated to Freddie and the Dreamers, Brian Poole and the Tremeloes, the Searchers, Dave Berry and his Cruisers, Tom Jones, Wayne Fontana and the Mindbenders and Gerry and the Pacemakers. It was all good stuff, though not all of them were as easy to handle as Billy.

Larry next asked me to manage a tour for Lonnie Donegan with Peter Goodwright, the impressionist, in support. Lonnie was a wonderful live act. For me he was a little short on charisma, but he made up for that with the energy of his songs and his skiffle routines.

Peter Goodwright was the godfather of impressionists. He specialised in the radio comics -Frankie Howerd, Ben Lyon, Jimmy Clitheroe, Al Read, Ted Ray, Hylda Baker. When you closed your eyes and listened it was as if they were in the room.

It was all great fun, but after a year of working for Larry Parnes, I was feeling jaded, run down and burned out. It was time for a holiday.

Chapter 7

Love in the wings

After the turmoil of Great Yarmouth, a seaside holiday in Eastbourne seemed the perfect antidote. I was feeling desperately tired, and all I wanted to do was rest. But when I met up with my friends Paula and Mike from the Morecambe and Wise panto, they handed me a ticket for the show they were appearing in.

I tried to explain that grateful as I was, this was the last thing I needed. They seemed a little surprised, but I think they understood.

I walked down the pier with them as far as the stage door, then found a quiet bench and sat down to look out over the sea and watch the fishermen.

It was a lovely evening with a light breeze and a clear blue sky. I could hear the Channel tide gently lapping the steel girders of the pier. I stared down between the boards to the sea underneath, feeling a welcome sense of peace.

An angler arrived and started setting up his tackle, and I got into a discussion with him about the ways of fish and fishermen. It was the first conversation I'd had in years that wasn't about the theatre. Just what I needed. I was unwinding already.

I must have nodded off, because the next thing I knew it was pitch dark. The show was over and the audience were piling out of the theatre. Paula and Mike stood in front of me.

Chapter 7

"Sorry!" I said. "I must have dropped off."

"Don't apologise" said Paula. "Come on round to the lounge bar and join us all for a drink."

I wasn't sure about this, but Paula insisted. She grabbed my arm and escorted me round the back of the theatre to the bar.

"Go and find a seat and I'll get you a Coke" she said. She knew I didn't drink alcohol.

I sat in a corner, well away from the dartboard and the juke box. Paula came back with my drink. With her was a young woman.

"This is my friend Annie" she said. "You don't mind if she sits with us?"

"Not at all" I said, although all I really wanted to do was go home and get some more sleep.

"Annie's one of the dancers in the show."

"That's nice" I smiled.

"John's just finished at Great Yarmouth with Billy Fury."

"Oh lovely, I think he's something else!" said Annie. Tired as I was, I couldn't help noticing that she was very attractive. She was petite and wore her dark hair in a fashionable beehive.

"Was he nice to work with?" she asked.

"Great" I said. I didn't mean to sound so flat, but I was having problems staying awake.

"I've heard him on the radio and they're always playing his records on the jukebox here" said my new friend. She paused, trying to think of something else to take the conversation forward.

Chapter 7

"Did you see the show tonight?" she asked.

"No, I'm afraid I didn't" I said. "I've spent so long in theatres that just now I need some breathing space."

I don't think Annie was too impressed. I assured her that I would love to see her show - just not until I'd had a few days' rest.

"Come before Thursday" she said. "We change programmes then and I won't have so much to do in the show after that."

I offered to walk her home, and we left Paula at the bar with a grin on her face. We chatted all the way there. She was certainly a delightful girl, and very easy to talk to. But I left her without making a firm arrangement to see her again.

Paula was not too happy with my lack of initiative, but I hadn't forgotten how good being with Annie had made me feel. She had a refreshingly untheatrical beauty. There was something very special about her.

I decided it was time to take the initiative. The next morning I went down to the pier and booked a seat at the front for that evening's performance. Then I bought a box of chocolates and some flowers and took them along to the stage door - early, so no-one would see me.

It was a full house that night. I enjoyed the show - it was all very traditional end-of-the-pier stuff - but I couldn't take my eyes off Annie. She was an excellent dancer, with a wonderful figure. In fact found it hard to look at anyone else.

I didn't go backstage after the show as I didn't want to push my luck, but I was dying to see her again.

The opportunity came soon enough. The company was going on a ghost-hunting evening at Pevensey Castle the following day, and Annie, I was told, had been thrilled by the chocolates and flowers and was insisting on my joining them.

The evening was great fun. Annie had made us a midnight picnic with half a bottle of wine for her and a soft drink for me.

I had to go home at the end of the week, and of course I missed Annie terribly. I phoned her backstage every night, hoping we would be able to see each other soon again. On her last night, I went back to Eastbourne without telling her and booked a front seat. That night I wound up escorting her to the town's 'Goodbye to the Cast' party.

The fact is, I suddenly wanted to be with Annie more than anyone else in the world. My feelings frightened me. I was terrified that someone else might snatch her away, yet at the same time I was aware that I must not scare her off. I didn't consider for a moment that she might have the same feelings for me.

To cut a long story short, I proposed to Annie at the end of the pier, and to my amazement, she accepted.

Annie had great difficulty explaining this to her father, who had sacrificed a great deal for her to succeed in the world of dance. He relied on his eldest daughter to balance a very difficult home life, and the thought of losing her was hard to accept. He gave her a terrible time over it, but she stood firm.

We were happy to agree to a twelve-month engagement. But my mother gave the marriage six months, and Annie's father prayed she would be proved right. Today, 42 happy years on, I'm pleased to say Mum is beginning to concede that we might have made the right decision. She adores Annie.

My next job was with a company called Neil Tuson Productions, a small but well respected conference organiser. They happened to need a dressmaker, and though she had never done this sort of work before, I persuaded Annie to give it a go. We needed to save all we could for our marriage.

The conferences were much smaller than the Mitchell Monkhouse events, but they were very professionally done. The work carried us through until it was panto time again.

Annie's role that season was in *Sleeping Beauty* at the Lyceum Theatre, Sheffield, starring an up-and-coming young comic called Roy Hudd. This meant she would be spending twelve weeks away from me in the depths of South Yorkshire - unthinkable! Fortunately Lawrence Green agreed to let me work on the panto, so we could look forward to being together at Christmas.

It came as a bit of a shock to Annie to see me stride into action as stage director of a big pantomime, and she found it difficult to be accepted by the other girls in the chorus once they knew she was engaged to the boss.

In Sheffield, for the second time in my pantomime career, I had to stand in for the star. Roy Hudd had got his feet badly burned trying to put out a fire in his child's nursery. Once again Annie looked on in amazement as I demonstrated my acting side.

I soon discovered Annie's extraordinary talent for dressmaking. She would outline a pattern on a sheet of brown paper, then create anything from an evening dress to a pair of trousers. Though she never bought any clothes from the shops, she always managed to look the smartest.

I can't write about our experiences in Sheffield without telling you about Mrs Evadne Broomhead. This was our improbably-named landlady at no. 17 London Road, Sheffield - without doubt the finest digs in the country.

Evadne was the stereotypical fire-breathing landlady, with support stockings, overalls under, a pinafore, a hairnet, thick glasses and huge slippers. She had a husband who was not allowed to speak, and a son of 40 who had never left home and spent his days sitting in the corner. Neither of them seemed to have anything to live for.

Mrs Broomhead had built herself a formidable reputation. Her prices were low and her portions were generous. She also looked after you very well and would do your laundry free of charge. We were allowed to take a bath on Sundays, but only after she had measured the depth of the water with a ruler.

By the time dinner was ready you could not see the person on the other side of the table. The roast dinners were the size of a three-tiered wedding cake. Breakfast was half a ton of mash, three sausages, three eggs, black pudding, mushrooms, beans and two pieces of doorstop bread. And you weren't allowed to leave any.

Mrs Broomhead had strict rules about hanky-panky between unmarried couples. We got caught late one evening as I tried to give Annie a piggyback on tiptoe up the stairs to my attic. I thought I could get away with it by avoiding the creaking stair, but Evadne was way ahead of me. She would readjust the boards so that different stairs creaked on different nights.

Annie's next dancing job was in the Dickie Henderson Show at the Britannia Pier in Great Yarmouth, where I had enjoyed such a successful season with Bob Monkhouse. So that we could again work in the same town, I agreed to take Larry Parnes' latest pop spectacular to the Royal Aquarium theatre opposite, where Billy Fury had been. This time a Liverpool band was topping the bill, Gerry and the Pacemakers.

But Annie and I had a little job to do before we started work on the two shows. Our year's engagement was up. We got married on May 19, 1967 at Wandsworth Registry Office, quickly and quietly without any fuss, in the company of our grieving relatives - except for my grandmother, who thought it was a joyous occasion.

Then it was back to Great Yarmouth for our honeymoon. We booked the honeymoon suite at The Sandringham Hotel, which was on the sea front, right opposite the two theatres.

We were shown our suite, all made ready for us with flowers and chocolates and a bottle of champagne in a bucket. This was our first night together - through all these months we had adhered to the old-fashioned demands of a Christian marriage.

We were still unpacking when there came a knock at the door - the hotel manager.

"I'm so sorry to bother you" he said. "I've been asked to see if you could pop over to your theatre before dinner and see Cecil, the resident stage manager."

He assured me that the request had sounded very urgent. Its timing could scarcely have been worse.

I crossed the road to the Royal Aquarium Theatre and began to vent my displeasure at the elderly Cecil, who worked as projectionist in the winter and resident stage manager in the summer.

Cecil explained that the scenery wouldn't fit. They had sent the Blackpool show instead of the Scarborough one, and they couldn't even get the set pieces through the door. And there was a revolving stage - something they had no experience of. The show was due to start in four days' time...

The poor man was now reduced to a gibbering heap of nerves. I thought I might easily wind up rushing him to the cardiac unit of the local hospital.

By now Annie had joined us. She understood that we had no choice.

Chapter 7

I rolled up my sleeves and worked all night to get that scenery in, then carried on for three days, day and night, with Annie bringing me flasks of coffee and Bovril to keep me going. She set up the wardrobe room and unpacked the costumes ready for the dancers. We got the show ready, but our honeymoon would have to wait. Thank goodness Annie understood.

The show opened successfully and on time. Our efforts did not go unappreciated. Larry Parnes showed his gratitude by placing a hefty cheque into our Post Office account "just to get us off the ground." And the owner of the Sandringham never charged us for the honeymoon suite - after all, we had never slept in it. Though Annie did manage to drink the champagne.

The silver screen

Now that I was married with responsibilities, my mother decided it was time to downsize, as they call it these days. She sold our Putney house at a considerable profit and bought a much smaller place in Shouldham Street, Marble Arch.

The location was a little too close to the city centre for my taste, but it did have a wonderful roof garden with a terrific view of London's skyline. Claude could now walk to work. Mother had just been appointed drama coach at The Royal Opera House in Convent Garden, so it was ideal for her too. They found Marie-Victoire, now twelve, a good school along the Edgware Road, and my grandmother accompanied her there each morning. My little sister showed great promise in art and was producing some exceptional works for her age.

My grandmother was not convinced about the wisdom of the move - until she found the Sue Ryder charity shop across the road. There was a sign in the window advertising for a mature woman for a managerial position. Nookie might have been in her eightieth year, but she didn't seem a day over 70 to us. She was perfect for the job, and the job was perfect for her.

People used to leave bags of things in the shop doorway in the dead of night, which sometimes led to ne'er-do-wells rummaging in the bags in the small hours to look for anything of value. They had reckoned without Nookie, who could see the shop from the house and didn't hesitate to let them know she was watching. She even invested in a powerful torch, which she would direct at the miscreants. Its lighthouse beam soon scared them off, though the neighbours didn't think much of it.

During the day she would sit behind her counter by the front door, a baseball bat under the counter in case of trouble. Sometimes my mother would join her to give her a hand. Nookie would talk the hind legs off a donkey with anyone who came in. Customers who had just popped in for a quick browse tended not to come back, but nobody left without buying something as that was the only way of being allowed out again.

Everyone soon learned about the baseball bat, and later the crowbar she added to her armoury. I don't think she ever actually used either of them, but then again nor did she ever get robbed.

Annie and I were booked for the Birmingham pantomime again, thankfully with Morecambe and Wise. I couldn't wait to introduce Annie to Eric and Ernie. We found digs in London Road, just a mile from the theatre.

It was another great panto, and a long and very successful run. This would be the pair's last panto as they wanted to concentrate on the television shows which would dominate the BBC's light entertainment schedules throughout the 1970s, most notably each Christmas Day. Christmas wasn't Christmas in those days without the *Morecambe and Wise Show.*

Eric called me into his dressing room one day for our weekly chat about 'Reluctant Matters of Interest and Little Consequence' as he used to call it.

"You should get into television, John" he told me. "It would be good for you at this stage of your career. You've had vast experience with all those years as a child actor and in theatre management - they'd be just what they're looking for.

"There's a man coming to see me tomorrow called Albert Knight. I want you to meet him, so make yourself available between houses tomorrow."

I was extremely grateful to Eric. He always made time to help those around him.

Eric kept his word. Albert Knight turned out to be the Grade Organisation's top producer. He was a charming man who spoke very quietly, and he put me at my ease immediately.

Albert complimented me on the smooth running of such a big production and said Eric thought highly of me. He asked me if I would consider going to Blackpool to stage-direct the summer show at the ABC Theatre. He would be producing it, and the line-up was Frank Ifield, Jimmy Tarbuck, The Barron Knights and Tania the Elephant.

But there was more. Every Sunday during the season, ABC Television would take over the theatre to produce a show called *Blackpool Night Out* for national transmission. The show would go out almost live, hitting the screens half an hour after it started, so the first half would be broadcast while the second half was still being shot. That year the TV line-up was to include, in addition to Eric and Ernie, Tom Jones, Dusty Springfield, Frank Sinatra junior, Mel Tormé, Frankie Howerd, Dickie Henderson, Tony Hancock and the Beatles. This really was big stuff.

The TV people were contracted to use the resident stage staff, which meant I would be running the shows alongside their floor manager. This would take me into television right at the top. On top of this, the TV contract would double my theatre salary each week.

I was frightened, flabbergasted - and delighted. I went straight back to Eric's room after Albert Knight had left and thanked him profusely.

"I know this will sound silly Eric, but could Annie and I take you out to dinner? Please!"

He looked at me and smiled. "Let's have a takeaway at my hotel. You can pay!"

That evening, Eric was the very first person to be told an important piece of news. Annie was pregnant. We had held it back in case they took Annie out of the chorus.

Annie's situation made it even more important to accept such a lucrative proposition. And I could see Eric's point of view - television had a huge future. I will always be grateful for his intervention.

It was a very long season, not least because the television input demanded a few weeks' extra preparation. I decided that we should go to Blackpool directly after the pantomime finished and set up a temporary home there.

Albert Knight had told me that it was time I signed up with an agent. I found an excellent one in Vincent Shaw, a large, rather temperamental man, but very well respected. Vincent was renowned for his hard negotiation skills and for looking after his clients with great loyalty. His big claim to fame was making a legend out of Sooty the puppet, with West End runs, TV shows, advertising - the lot. I would be delighted if he could do for John Stirling what he had done for Sooty.

Vincent Shaw negotiated my Blackpool contract, and it was such a good deal that I think Albert may have regretted advising me to get an agent!

Annie had made the acquaintance of two elderly costumiers who worked for Albert, Winnie Gill and her assistant Thelma. They had been brought over from Australia to design and make costumes for all the big shows. Their pedigree stretched from Las Vegas to the Folies Bergères and Broadway. Winnie and Thelma were the queens of glitter, feathers and sequins. They saw an opening for Annie and asked her to join them in their new costume house back in London.

Chapter 8

Annie adored Winnie and Thelma, and they felt the same way about her. They soon found that Annie's skills were exceptional. They would have liked to nurse her along, but the instant success of the costumes forced her straight in at the deep end. Fortunately she was very fit and healthy and never suffered from morning sickness.

Naturally I wanted Annie in Blackpool for the summer, where she could be close to me. So they made her wardrobe mistress for both the summer show and the television shows.

The baby was due in September, on the last night of the summer show, so we had the whole season to get through.

Albert Knight phoned me as soon as I got settled in Blackpool. "Have you met Jim Smith yet?" Jim was the resident projectionist - the ABC was a cinema in the winter months. I hadn't. I wondered why he was asking.

"You'd better ask him where you're going to put the elephant. It's arriving in Blackpool from Las Vegas next Tuesday."

I trotted off to see Jim. My first idea was that as Blackpool had its own Tower Circus, with five elephants in residence, Tania could have slipped in there practically unnoticed. But her keeper blew a fuse at that idea. Didn't we realise that Tania was an artiste? She would need her own dressing room and space!

Jim and I decided to convert the dock bay at the back of the theatre into a temporary elephant house.

My first foray into television proved quite a challenge. Banks and banks of lighting had to be fitted up overnight after the Saturday theatre show had finished. The orchestra pit had to be augmented to house Bob Sharples' 60-piece orchestra. A new Formica floor had to be laid overnight and a revolving stage put in. Everything was so different from the weekly show - yet it all had to be put back every Sunday night for the stage show to re-open on the Monday. We didn't get much sleep from Saturday lunchtime until midnight on the Monday. Now we knew why they were prepared to pay us so much.

Blackpool Night Out was broadcast at 8pm on Sundays, replacing *Sunday Night at the Palladium*. We were able to get the first half hour in the can in case there were any problems.

It wasn't long before we hit a big one. Tony Hancock was taken ill and was unable to host the show. He was suffering from depression and on strong medication. So Dickie Henderson stepped in.

As Dickie walked on to the stage there was a huge crash backstage. An arc lamp had fallen from the ceiling and hit a stage hand.

It was an extremely serious injury; half the man's face had been torn away. Dickie, hearing the crash, made a joke out of it - and looked through the curtain to see what had happened. The sight he was faced with was horrific. There was blood everywhere and the poor man was screaming and in terrible pain.

Dickie was severely shaken, but like a true professional he overcame the experience and carried on with the show. He saw it as his duty not to frighten the audience but to calm the situation.

And then there came a scream from the side of the stage. Frankie Howerd had been waiting to enter from the wings when the elephant decided to stand on his foot.

Fortunately we intervened in time to pull Frankie's foot out of the shoe before it was crushed. The shoe, however, was rammed right into the stage, and nobody could get it out.

Frankie walked to the centre of the stage limping and with one shoe missing. "What happened?" Dickie asked. "The elephant stood on my foot" said Frankie. "You hum it, I'll play it" said Dickie. At this stage we were only ten minutes away from going live to the nation.

Dusty Springfield, as our top of the bill, was waiting to go on. Dusty did not like problems and surprises, but she managed to keep calm and avoid the elephant. The public never found out what had happened, and the audience at home got a first class show. We, on the other hand, were close to being sectioned.

That was my initiation to television, and in a single hour a man had been critically hurt, Frankie Howerd had come near to losing his foot, an elephant was out of control and a famous singer was in a bad temper. I began to wonder if I would be able to stand the pace.

I need not have worried. The rest of the shows worked like clockwork. Mel Tormé was especially impressive to watch as he rehearsed his orchestra - that was a lesson in itself. At one point he stopped them in full flight and said quietly "Third trombone - that wasn't quite right." Quite extraordinary.

The Beatles were great fun. Even with all their security around them, they said hello to everyone. They were very buoyed up with energy and excitement, which made their performance very sharp and entertaining.

The last night of the summer season arrived and still there was no sign of our baby. Everyone went home, leaving us both feeling very alone. We moved into a B&B as our flat had to be vacated. Two more weeks went by before the doctors decided it was time to induce.

I had generally been ok at handling panics of various kinds, and I'd become well used to dealing with things that weren't supposed to happen. But this time I was being tested to the limit. I was being asked to time

Chapter 8

Annie's contractions and record each one by reference to the giant hospital clock on the wall in front of her bed.

The delivery room was not the friendliest place I had been in, and Annie was now screaming quite a lot, which to say the least was unsettling. She was now in great pain and her labour was taking a very long time. After twelve hours, the contractions were coming fast and furious. I realised that I wasn't feeling too good either - the circulation in both my hands had gone.

I'm ashamed to say that just before the critical moment came I fainted and had to be carried from the room. To this day I will never forgive myself for leaving my sweet Annie at that time.

But little Mark Stirling had arrived, all nine and a half pounds of him, and every finger and toe present and correct. We were overjoyed, though Annie made me swear on the Bible that I would never, ever let it happen again.

On the Street

There was great sadness when Alzheimer's Disease claimed my beloved Auntie Nellie in 1969. Her legacy to my mother was her house in Edgware, Middlesex, and as Annie, Mark and I did not yet have anywhere to live, we moved in.

It was a lovely house, with a rock garden and a fish pond at the front and a big bay window overlooking the tree-lined avenue. The front was beautifully decorated by cherry trees, though the back was rather less attractive at times as it backed on to the Edgware underground terminus and we would often find rubbish from the trains on the lawn.

One day my agent, Vincent Shaw, called me in for a chat about my future. He told me that he had been doing some thinking. Granada Television in Manchester was looking for an assistant stage manager, he said.

That didn't sound too good, I thought - a backward step, surely?

Vincent saw my alarm. "It's very different from what you've been used to John, but it's a foot in the door of something you need to achieve. You'll be responsible to the producer and director for the overall script - all the cuts, the changes, the moves, the continuity. You'll hold the master copy for everyone to check with.

"It has to be done well - and if it is, it'll be the first step on the ladder to becoming a researcher, a director and finally a producer. If you work hard it doesn't take that long - I've had people promoted to the top jobs within 18 months."

And then Vincent told me which show I'd be working on.

Coronation Street!

At that time 'The Street' was pulling in nineteen million avid fans each week, and I was one of them. Half of me was thrilled at the prospect, while the other half was numb with shock. To me, as to so many, the people of *Coronation Street* were real. I didn't want the illusion shattered.

I arrived at Granada Television in Quay Street, Manchester, at 9.30 on a Monday morning. The floor manager, Colin McIntyre, and a lovely production assistant called Sue took me down to the rehearsal room. It was like a police escort. I was clutching my new blue WH Smith script holder, along with two scripts I had just been given. We came to a hall outside the rehearsal room door.

"Take a deep breath," said Colin with a wink. "They won't bite." We went through the swing doors into a rehearsal room, otherwise known as the Green Room.

I left behind the real world - and entered the portals of fantasy. It was like being shown one of the Seven Wonders of the World. Elsie Tanner, Ken Barlow, Annie Walker, Stan Ogden - every time I blinked, another household name seemed to stroll in.

The floor of the Green Room was marked in sections, each depicting part of the set - the Rovers Return, the Ogden's house, Elsie Tanner's Living Room, Len Fairclough's building yard. At one end were two more rooms. One was for the men, with a green baize card table in the middle, a dartboard, a copy of *Racing Times* and a quantity of Vernon's Pools coupons. The other was lined with embroidered armchairs and had lots of cushions, pretty pictures on the wall, a noticeboard plastered with cards and letters from fans. This was the Ladies' Castle.

As their scenes were duly marked and rehearsed, the cast would head for their respective rest rooms. There was the Pat Phoenix corner, The Ogdens' corner and the Royal Box corner, the domain of Doris Speed, who played Annie Walker. The last corner belonged to Jack Howarth (Albert Tatlock) and Margot Bryant (Minnie Caldwell) near to the door. This was a strategic move, as they had to be near the tea trolley when it came in. There were only so many of each kind of cream cake, and Jack's strategy was to strike like lightning to secure his favourite before anyone else had a chance.

Colin went to great lengths to teach me how to cajole these household names into doing their scenes promptly as they came up. "They never listen for a call - they've been doing it for so long" he said. "They shut themselves away in their little worlds until you go and get them. One of your jobs is to make sure they are standing by for the next scene."

He explained that it was no good just shouting a name and leaving the room - it wouldn't work.

"First, be polite and remind them that their scene is coming up. Then you stand over them until they actually move into the rehearsal room, then you follow. They're all extremely professional and hardly ever cause problems, but they do tend to jump on newcomers and try and give them the run around - it's all part of working on the Street."

The cast appeared to have arranged themselves in separate camps in order of supremacy - and I began to understand why. If you're in a show that runs this long, you can imagine how much space they need if everyone is going to get along. So the separation between scenes was beautifully executed.

Chapter 9

"You must remember that at all times the show is the star attraction. Everybody just works to that end - however they may behave" whispered that week's writer, Geoffrey Lancashire, as I began to mark in the cuts and changes. I could see Geoffrey squirm from time to time as lines which he had slaved over were brutally cut out. He would fight his corner now and again to retain the speeches which he felt were vital to the scenes.

There was a readthrough, then the cast and the director went into a process known as 'blocking it', which meant bringing the script to life with the right moves, props and so on. After that I had to start running around like a headless chicken to try to get the cast ready for their scenes. That was when I met my first challenge.

I walked into the men's rest room, where six of them were hunched over the little card table with their hands of cards at the ready. It was a game of poker.

I announced the names of the actors who were needed. They didn't even bother to look up. "Hold your horses" one of them grunted. I stood my ground as I had been instructed, and waited for the men I had called to stand up and head for the door.

Nothing happened. For all the notice they were taking of me, I might as well have been a stain on the carpet.

Now what to do? I could hardly go back into the rehearsal room on my very first day and tell the director he would have to wait. I appealed to Colin.

"Watch me" he said. He stood in the open doorway of the rest room and in a loud and authoritative voice shouted out: "Scene 4 - Bill, Bernard, Jack, Tom and Peter! Gentlemen, we are waiting to continue our rehearsal with you please, now this minute."

They all put down their cards, rather begrudgingly (face down of course),

Chapter 9

and went through the door to begin the rehearsal.

I soon got to know the foibles of the Street's stars. Pat Phoenix always seemed to be on an important phone call. Doris Speed never had to be called at all, but she didn't like being kept waiting by anyone.

I felt sorry that week for two actresses who had come in from the cold to play small but to them crucial parts. They were given no slack. One made the mistake of going to the toilet just as we were getting to her scene. When she walked back in, the whole rehearsal room went silent. She didn't make that mistake again.

I began to realise that the Green Room was a kind of sanctuary for the regulars - a haven where they could get their personal business done and catch up with each other's news. It was a rare chance to get out of the public eye.

After three and a half days' rehearsal, it was time to go down to studio 8 and rehearse and record the two episodes in front of the cameras. One episode was done in the morning, the second in the afternoon. My master script had changed from blue to yellow to indicate that it was now a camera script.

At this stage I was given a 'cut key', a long piece of cable with a button on one end. The cable went right round the studio with me and I had to be careful not to get it caught up somewhere. If an artist forgot a line, my job was to immediately press the button, which cut off the sound and allowed the actor to be given a prompt without it being recorded. This was of course only for use when necessary, and the button must never be held down for longer than five seconds or the scene would be ruined.

I didn't have to use the cut key very often. The best course was to give the veterans every chance to get themselves out of trouble without help, and they nearly always did. Sometimes another actor would take the line and carry the scene on.

Chapter 9

Unfortunately on my first outing I had to work on an awkward episode, in which Pat Phoenix and Alan Browning had several very long scenes together. There was an awful lot for them to remember and I had to use my cut key four times. Happily, both Pat and Alan took their prompts straight away. The scenes were not affected and the viewers noticed nothing.

Some of the cast were grateful for the prompt and felt a certain security knowing I was there with my button if needed. Others, however, were angry, with themselves mainly - but they would direct their anger at me. "Have you never heard of a dramatic pause?" they would say, or "You didn't have to spoil my timing." Or they would simply deny flat out that they had 'dried'.

Coronation Street was a world of its own, and I revelled in the job. In my six months on the show I became good friends with most of the cast. They were like one very special happy family. The artists had great respect for each other, and we had the pleasure of brilliant scripts from writers as talented as Geoffrey Lancashire and Jack Rosenthal. I learned a huge amount from all of them.

Yet I have to say that the memory that will take longest to fade is Jack Howarth and the speed with which he could raid the four o'clock tea trolley. Jack was the oldest member of the company - well into his eighties - but when that trolley entered the rehearsal room he would have made a gazelle look slow.

His ingenuity on the set impressed me almost as much. As Albert Tatlock he could break away from a scene to collect a chocolate éclair, then continue his lines without anybody noticing that he had departed from the script.

On Friday nights, the second episode had to be in the can by 6.30 - otherwise those of us who were travelling home to London would miss the

7.35 from Piccadilly. So as soon as we got the all clear, there was a mass charge for the line of taxis waiting outside the studios. If an actor made a mistake and scenes had to be re-recorded, we'd have to miss the train and the offending performer would be sent to Coventry for some time. Fortunately that didn't happen very often.

There was some debate with Annie about what to do when my six months on the Street were up. It wasn't much fun being in Manchester all week with Annie being left alone to look after little Mark. At the same time, working at Granada promised an important foot up the ladder and greater security for all of us.

So we agreed I should carry on. Vincent Shaw accepted another six-month contract with a written promise that I be considered for promotion at the end of it.

On my return to Manchester, I was seconded to the drama department to work on Granada's biggest drama series for some time. It was called *A Family at War,* and it was going to be three years in the making.

Colin Douglas played the head of the family and Sheelagh Frazer was his wife. Unfortunately Colin and Sheelagh did not get on very well and it started to look like hard work. It was the devil's own work to keep a foot in both camps, and some of the arguments were very heated.

To film the beach scenes, Granada took sand to the coastal resort of Formby to fill up the existing dunes and make a nice long straight beach. In France we had to shoot some flying scenes. Flying a rust-bucket with the film cameraman literally hanging out of the door by his braces was not an experience I ever want to repeat.

Many artists started their acting careers in 'Family', notably Nigel Hawthorne, Richard Easton, Barbara Flynn, Coral Atkins, Maureen

Lipman and Julie Goodyear, plus my favourite, Lynda Bellingham.

My contract was renewed for a year, with the position of researcher promised at the end of it. Colin Douglas, bless him, had insisted I stay with the show. The first series of *A Family at War* reached the top of the ratings, and two more followed.

I worried about Annie terribly. She was now at the ABC theatre in Great Yarmouth, looking after the costumes for Albert Knight. It was a long drive from Manchester to Great Yarmouth. Her show featured Engelbert Humperdinck, Freddie Starr and Basil Brush. Mark was with Annie, and adored his evening chats in the wardrobe with Basil Brush. Ivan Owen, the voice of Basil, always made plenty of time for Mark.

I felt an urge to spread my wings a little and get involved in other shows that were going into production at the studios. The show I really wanted to be a part of was *The Lovers*, written by Jack Rosenthal and directed by the up-and-coming Michael Apted. Paula Wilcox and Richard Beckinsale were the two star-crossed lovers with Maureen Lipman (Jack's wife) and Robin Nedwell as their friends.

I had already had the immense pleasure of working on several of Jack Rosenthal's episodes of *Coronation Street*. I had always kept his scripts, as they were so special. Jack would cram so much into a half-hour script. I was a huge fan of his, and I'm pleased to say he was a charming and modest man to work for.

The Lovers was a big success. We did two series before Richard and Paula decided it was time to move on - both were in great demand. It was a terrible tragedy that Richard died so suddenly when he was only 31.

Jack Rosenthal advised me to keep my eye on the vacancies posted on Granada's notice board. He suggested I apply for a position which had come up as promotion scriptwriter - that was where he had started. I did as he suggested and got the job, which rather irritated Vincent.

For this post I joined another young man called Rick Vaines, a very funny man with his roots and accent deeply entrenched in Oldham. Rick was immensely amusing, very slick, and was already making terrific promotional clips. I decided to stay behind him for a while to learn the ropes. This was a job I had never done before, but Rick was very generous and made me feel immediately that I had something to contribute.

We had to prepare three to four-minute promotions using clips from the shows, writing editorials to go with them. The aim was to stop viewers switching to another channel. We would spend hours in the editing suite watching footage from the shows, trying to select the clips that would keep the viewer hooked.

Next I became a researcher on a series called *Adam Smith*, about a Scottish minister in Glasgow's Gorbals. It was excellent, but it wasn't my bag at all. I didn't do well on it, and I told them I would prefer not to do the second series. They didn't mind.

After four and a half happy years in Manchester I was beginning to think about returning home. But then Johnny Hamp, Head of Light Entertainment, asked me to join his production team as a research assistant looking for new talent, as well as established acts who had not, as yet, had much television exposure.

This was the side of the business I had always wanted to get into, and Vincent Shaw agreed that I should take the job. Annie and Mark moved up to join me and we rented a flat in Cheadle Hulme. Annie was immediately offered three costume jobs - and unbelievably, she accepted all three. One was with the Royal Exchange theatre company, one on a new series of *The Good Old Days* and the other on a new series of *Sunday Night at the London Palladium*.

She brought in a cutter to help her on the last of these each week, as she had to make more than 40 costumes for a group of dancers called *The Second Generation*. She would start them on Mondays at the Palladium, then rush back on the train, sew them all together and return to Manchester each Thursday for fittings. Then she'd be back on the train to finish them all off and back up in time dress rehearsal. Fortunately they gave her more time for *The Good Old Days*, where she made costumes for artists like Danny La Rue and John Inman.

The Royal Exchange then offered Annie a permanent position in charge of their wardrobe. That led to her working with some big names in the theatre - Albert Finney, Michael Hordern, Edward Fox, Vanessa Redgrave and Tom Courtenay.

Granada was generally acclaimed as the leading station for drama, thanks to blockbusters like *Brideshead Revisited* and *The Jewel in the Crown*. Light entertainment was not so high on its list of priorities and Johnny Hamp had a battle on his hands to get the department properly recognised. But Johnny managed to put his own mark on the channel. In 1971 he gave Granada the cheapest show in the history of television, and at the same time one of its biggest hits - *The Comedians*.

The format could not have been simpler. Johnny would put seven stand-up comics in a small studio with an invited audience. He would get each comic to do 20 minutes, then edit short extracts together. Johnny was a master in the editing suite. He would spend days finding the best way to link the material.

My job was to travel the country in search of comedians who were new, original and most important of all, funny. I spent night after night sitting in smoky working men's clubs searching for the nuggets of gold among the dross. It was hard work - for every comic who made me laugh, there were a hundred who didn't.

Chapter 9

If a comedian knew I was in the audience, he would often feel he had to do an hour instead of ten minutes. That was a big mistake. The cleverer ones just gave you a taster and left the rest to your imagination. We picked out Ken Goodwin, Charlie Williams, George Roper, Duggie Brown, Frank Carson and Bernard Manning. I found Asian comics, African comics, Jewish comics - even, eventually, one or two female comics.

The series was a huge success. It went on to run for 22 years, and I hate to think how many comics appeared on it in total. The best of them became household names - some of them still are.

Johnny Hamp then took the concept one stage further by building a replica of a working men's club at Granada Studios. He called it *The Wheeltappers' and Shunters' Social Club*. The chairman, Colin Crompton, with his flat hat and an enormous bell, presided over the show with down-to-earth announcements such as "The pies are coming without mushy peas tonight".

Bernard Manning was our compère - very funny, though he could be cruel to the acts. Much of his material was too filthy to broadcast, but Johnny got round this in the editing suite by attaching a laugh from a dirty gag to the end of a clean one.

We invited acts from overseas who would never dream of appearing in such a setting in real life - Buddy Greco, Howard Keel and the Three Degrees, who made their TV debut on *Wheeltappers*. Closer to home there was Dusty Springfield (the only act for whom Bernard moderated his material), Kathy Kirby, Lonnie Donegan, Peters and Lee, Cannon and Ball and the Grumbleweeds. Paul Daniels started his TV career on the show.

The success of *Wheeltappers* kept me out on the road for long weeks looking for the right performers. It was a demanding job with extremely long hours and a great deal of travelling, but I revelled in it.

Chapter 9

Working for Johnny Hamp was a wonderful experience, but I was now keen to start producing light entertainment shows. I left Granada in 1976 after seven happy years. Vincent wasn't sure I was making the right decision, but he gave me his full support.

I set up my own production office in King Street, Manchester, with the aim of trying to produce my own series - not just for TV but for cabaret and theatre. Huge cabaret clubs were sprouting up all over the country, and it was a medium I very much wanted to get into. I wanted to do live concerts and floor shows and produce great sets.

My venture paid off. I did floor shows at most of the leading cabaret clubs, both in the UK and overseas. I was able to produce shows with comics like Pat Daniels and Cannon and Ball. I found myself producing sequences for television shows like *The Generation Game.* I went abroad and brought back overseas acts for shows here. I did *Game For A Laugh* and *the Royal Variety Performance.* I even became the talent co-ordinator at London Weekend Television.

It was all going very well, but I felt I was playing rather than working. I was not carving out a career for myself. So I decided to take a gap year to think about it. I took Annie and Mark and six dancers to Malta, where for six months we did our own floor show at an open air amphitheatre called the Buskett Roadhouse. Frankly, this was a glorified holiday, but one Annie and I badly needed.

After Malta we spent three months in Brussels, appearing at a city centre night spot called Chez Paul. It was wonderful - we'd have eight internationally-known acts one after the other, from jugglers to dogs and budgerigars. I finished off the year by appearing in a double act with a dancer, Diane Massey. Annie made some stunning costumes for her.

My break had blown away the cobwebs and satisfied my urge to perform.

Chapter 9

I felt I could now settle down and do some real work.

Back home, I set out on one of my weekend drives to join Annie and Mark in Great Yarmouth, where she was in charge of *The Engelbert Humperdinck Show*. I left Manchester at seven in the evening and motored steadily across country through Chesterfield, Mansfield, and Grantham and on towards Norfolk.

Around 11 pm I reached a little village called Beeston and took the turning for Norwich across an Army bridge. The road ran straight in front of me, so I put my foot down. I was looking forward to getting home to my loved ones.

I had no way of knowing that a few minutes before, a lorry had shed its load of diesel across that road. I must have hit the oil at well over 60 miles an hour. I struggled with the steering wheel, but it no longer seemed to be connected to the rest of the car. Nor did the brakes.

In an instant I found myself a helpless passenger. Utterly out of control, the car shot off the road to the right and ploughed headlong into a fence. The engine smashed through the windscreen, and a concrete post came straight through the left side of the car and carried the seat out through the back.

The car turned over and over and over - four times, I think - then plunged down a gully into a field of strawberries. It finished upside down, the wheels spinning gradually to a stop.

I lay there for a few moments, wondering whether I was dead or merely dying. I couldn't move anything, because I was pinned down by the radiator. I couldn't feel any great pain, except in my back.

No-one seemed to have heard the crash - no-one came to help. And no-one would be able to see me if they did come past, because I was down in a ditch. I began to tremble with shock, cold and fear. Then I started passing out. I hadn't died yet, but it was clear that I very soon would.

Two and a half hours went by like this before I heard voices. It was a local farmer and his wife. They crawled down the bank and apologised for keeping me waiting - they had been afraid of intervening because it looked like such a bad accident.

They called an ambulance, and the ambulance team called the Fire Brigade. It took them an hour to get me out.

In the ambulance, two wonderful paramedics checked me over. Neither they nor the firemen could believe I had got off so lightly - my only injury was a big bruise on my back. They called Annie to tell her what had happened, and the ambulance whisked me off to Yarmouth General Hospital. Annie met me there, tearful and worried out of her mind, but relieved to see I was in one piece.

The next day the fun started. I couldn't stop reliving the accident. Every time I closed my eyes I felt I was somersaulting down that bank all over again. I fainted several times during the day and my nerves were all over the place.

But I got over it all in the end. And something very positive came from that accident - a total determination not to mess around with my career any more. Life was too short. I was going to tackle some serious work, and some worthwhile producing. If possible, I was going to put on my own musical.

Juliet Mills (left) and Hayley (right) with John and Muffin the Mule

Annie the dancer

Annie in the chorus line (right)

Annie the costumier

Sister Marie-Victoire

Aunt Monica the writer

John & his Ford Cortina

John & Annie getting married

Dame Judi Dench

The cast of Once in a Lifetime including Mark Stirling (far right)

Marti Caine

Marti Caine & the cast of Once in a Lifetime

Mark Stirling

Mark the skier...

...and tennis player

Annie, Judi and John at Judi's home

John with his mother and stepfather Claude at Pictor Hall

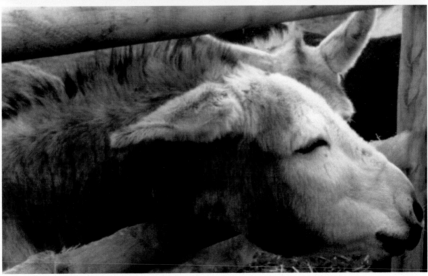

Chapter 10

The crest of a wave

During our travels through this complex, inspiring and unpredictable business of ours, we are sometimes asked to do certain things out of the blue - extraordinary things, things that usually have little or nothing to do with our normal jobs.

Peter Hall, an old friend of ours, was a floor manager at ABC Television in Birmingham - I had noticed his name on the credits of ABC's show *New Faces*. He, in turn, had read an article I had written for *The Stage* attacking the show for its policy of auditioning and publicly slaughtering new performers in front of a TV audience of millions, often with judges who didn't know what they were talking about. Though a few exceptional acts went on to become household names, hundreds suffered terrible consequences and found themselves without work. My article caused a furore.

I had first worked with Peter when we were both junior stagehands at the Golders Green Hippodrome. Each year we would get involved with the annual *Gang Show*, which Ralph Reader used to present at the theatre. Peter had been a Scout leader, so he had become closely involved in the movement.

In 1976, Birmingham's *Gang Show* was to feature Girl Guides as well as Scouts for the first time. This was a great relief to the boys, who would not have to dress up as girls any more, but as Peter explained to me, it posed a bit of a headache with the choreography.

When I told him Annie had been a dancer, his face lit up. "We desperately need a choreographer to knock out a couple of numbers for this year's gang show" he said. "It's very simple, but as we have Guides for the first time we feel the dance routines need stepping up. Would you help us out?" He looked at her pleadingly. She couldn't refuse.

The job involved rehearsing every weekend for three months. 300 Scouts and 120 Guides, plus Beavers, Cubs and Brownies, were all crammed into a little Scout hut on the suburbs of Birmingham. I have never heard a noise like it. The Scoutmasters and Brown Owls all lost their voices the first weekend, just trying to get some semblance of order.

The musical director, Peter Harris, played the piano and wrote the arrangements. When the noise got intolerable he would slam the lid of the piano down with a crash and scream for silence, which worked for about three minutes. I believe he got through four piano lids.

There was fierce rivalry for spots, and the old guard would not give an inch to the younger ones. Annie struggled hard to work out professional routines for people who did not know their left feet from their right, but somehow she managed it.

At the end of the show Peter Hall asked Annie if she would agree to do the all important Silver Jubilee Gang Show the following year, to celebrate the Queen's Anniversary. She said she would do it as long her health and sanity remained intact.

Peter Harris couldn't do this show as he was committed to working on the Muppets' first feature film, so they needed someone else to direct.

At that time I was in the middle of producing a stage act for Cannon and Ball, who were just hitting the big time. The boys had been hugely successful in night clubs, but they were now ready to march into television. They wanted to bring a new dimension to their act, watering down the colloquial Northern humour with comedy designed to appeal to a wider TV audience.

Peter Hall called me to ask if I would consider taking Peter Harris' place. I had severe doubts about this; I did not have anything like Peter's musical accomplishments. Nor could I write sketches or production numbers as he had. So I did not feel I could follow in his footsteps, particularly on such a big occasion.

I asked Peter to call an extraordinary meeting of the Scout and Guide leaders to talk about the problem. I explained that I appreciated the need to keep the show in line with Ralph Reader's heritage. But I felt that like most things, it had to be brought into the modern era - something which would clearly come as a terrible shock to the stalwarts. They were still coming to terms with having Girl Guides in the show.

I wanted to get rid of all the similarities to panto, both visually with the backcloths and musically with the standard production numbers. I told them I could not possibly follow in Peter Harris' footsteps, nor did I intend to try - I would have to do it my way.

I explained that I would need a standing set with no cloths of any sort, so that when the audience came into the theatre they would be faced with the set. The curtain would not fall at the end of the show - the performers would simply leave the stage. And there would be no stagehands - most of the changes would be made in full view of the audience by the Scouts themselves. There would be an elaborate lighting gantry, and I would need a good theatre designer to develop a new theme and a fresh setting.

Having dropped this bombshell on their lap I returned to Manchester and Cannon and Ball. I didn't expect to hear from the Scouts again - but to

Chapter 10

my surprise, they decided to go with my plan.

My sister Marie-Victoire had now left Wimbledon Art College with high recommendations and her scenic designs were going down very well in regional theatres. She was working on shows like *West Side Story,* as well as some obscure plays which needed all her concentration and talent. I asked her if there was any chance that she'd be able to work with me on *The Gang Show.*

She was surprised to be asked this, as we had never considered working together before. But the Birmingham Hippodrome was a big theatre, well respected by most touring managers, and my free-standing permanent set with modernistic lighting gantry appealed to her.

Marie-Victoire came up with a miraculous concept. The entire set would be made of scaffolding, painted in a variety of pastel shades. She put in ramps and built a bridge which went right across the stage. The scaffolding was three levels high, with all sorts of ingenious entrances and exit points. The builders in the Scout movement helped enormously by donating boards of every size. It was very modern, and to the Scouts looking at the finished product, very scary. But when the gantry was up and the lamps in place, it was a work of genius.

The set would transform itself from a playground to the deck of a ship, from a wood to a church. The combination of scaffolding and lighting turned out to be a magical combination, unseen in the theatre before. The audience was spellbound. Marie-Victoire got tremendous acclaim for her vision.

The show was fast moving, with no breaks for scene changes. The young Scouts and Guides took to it like ducks to water, and each night they received a standing ovation. The older Scouts might have felt a little sidelined, but they seemed to accept the need to give way to the younger generation and to a more modern approach.

Chapter 10

Unfortunately, by the time the next *Gang Show* came round, our approach had been quietly buried. The show went back to its old ways. I could see why they had done it, but naturally I was disappointed. I have no regrets, however. Both Mairie-Victoire and I received a lot of acclaim from the industry for it, and Annie was fêted for her original costumes.

I like to think that Ralph Reader would have enjoyed our show. No doubt he would have changed a few things, but I believe he would have accepted the need to move the *Gang Show* into the modern age.

Chapter 11

Marti

The decision in 1980 to embark on a production of my own was a big one, not least because of the risk I knew I'd be taking for myself and my family. I had to create a production, find a theme, write a show, cast it, direct it, and most daunting of all, somehow pay for it.

But first I had to find a very special star to front it - an artist who was as much at home singing as dancing, who could act and make people laugh. I had in mind one very special performer who would fit the bill perfectly – Marti Caine. But would Marti agree to working with me?

Some years before, I had written an article for *The Stage* attacking the ABC talent show *New Faces* for its policy of auditioning and often publicly slaughtering new performers in front of a TV audience of millions. I complained that many of the judges didn't know what they were talking about. Though a few exceptional acts went on to become household names, hundreds suffered terrible consequences and found themselves out of work. My article caused a furore. Unfortunately Marti was one of those who had made it to the top through *New Faces*.

In fact I had known Marti before she appeared in *New Faces* in 1975, thanks to my travels for Granada. I had often called into a nightclub called the Aquarius on the outskirts of Chesterfield, where she was the compère. Marti had shone above the rest of the performers. Since she had hit the big time she had played in Las Vegas, New York, South Africa and Canada as well as all over the UK. Now she had her own television show.

I put my idea first to her manager, Johnny Peller. I knew Johnny made all the decisions and Marti rarely questioned his judgement. Fortunately Johnny saw the potential of my plan, and agreed that Marti was the right woman for the job.

Johnny put the proposition to Marti. No problem there, she was happy to trust his judgment. It took me longer to arrange a meeting with Marti herself – she didn't like getting involved in business discussions – but I felt it was essential that we discuss my plans face to face, as I needed her input and her ideas.

We met Marti in her high-rise apartment overlooking the city lights of Sheffield, her home city. In person she was delightful, funny and mischievous. She seemed very enthusiastic about the project.

"That doesn't mean she's going to do it" Johnny warned me. "She's enthusiastic about lots of offers, but she can't possibly do them all."

We sat down and I brought out my designs and plans for the production. Marti spread them over her enormous coffee table, sat on the floor, kicked off her shoes and started to look through them.

"Wow!" she said. "You've really done your homework. Are you sure it's me you want to do this show for you?"

"I can't contemplate doing it without you" I said. I meant it.

"I think it's exactly what you need just now" said Johnny.

I threw in a few additional details to help her to make her mind up. I told her I had already contacted Willie Hurst, who had looked after the music for all Marti's big shows, to put together an orchestra of her favourite musicians. That went down well. Finally, I revealed where I was proposing to put on the show at the City Hall in her own beloved Sheffield, for four weeks over Christmas. Johnny told her we were planning ten shows to a week to cover the costs.

"That's a big commitment Johnny, with all the other things over Christmas" Marti said. I held my breath.

"It's totally original. You'll be the first to tackle a show like this" said Johnny.

"Two shows a day?" she stared at me.

"Two shows a day" I said.

"Do you think we'll get decent houses?"

"It's a risk for all of us" said Johnny. "If we don't fill the theatre, people will say you can't get big audiences. But I believe you can - you ARE Sheffield. They adore you here.

"For John, his reputation is on the line. If he is willing to try this then so should we."

"OK" she said. "I'll do your show John, God help us all." She turned to Johnny. "Over to you, Batman - do the business! I'll make the tea."

She never even mentioned *New Faces*.

Marti saw the look of utter relief on my face. I'm not usually an emotional man, but just now I was close to tears. It meant so much to me to have the artist I most wanted for my project.

Marti got up from the floor, came over to me and gave me a huge hug. "We'll do it together, OK?" she whispered.

The working title for the show was *Once In A Lifetime*. That was exactly what I wanted it to be - a once-in-a-lifetime experience for everyone associated with this very special venture.

I told Marti and John I planned to find 40 children between the ages of eight and fourteen to form the heart of the show. They would dance and sing with Marti and be a part of her sketches and comedy pieces. I had already begun the selection process, and I'd been overwhelmed by the talent I had found. I told Marti I had approached a choreographer called Judith Sylvester – she knew Judith and agreed she was the best.

It would be a two-and-a-half-hour concert with a 20-minute interval. There would be an open concert platform, without scenery - the stage was too big – but with an enormous lighting gantry. The children would have ten changes of costume each and she would have sixteen. We would have to rehearse with the children for up to three months.

"One thing, John" said Marti. "This is my home town, my own people. They like to think Sheffield owns me – and they're right. I have to come across as one of them, the local girl who made good.

"I'm very proud of Sheffield and I don't want to let them down. This has to be a success."

I said I understood.

I went away from her flat walking on air. I placed ads in the *Sheffield Echo* and the *Sheffield Star* appealing for talented children who would like the opportunity of working with Marti in her new Christmas Show at the City Hall. All they had to do for the audition was learn one song, one which was riding high in the charts - *Matchstalk Men and Matchstalk Cats and Dogs*, written by a duo called Brian and Michael about the paintings of L S Lowry. The ad stipulated that those who came to be auditioned must know the song off by heart. Otherwise – they simply needed talent.

Chapter 11

What happened next was unbelievable.

I arrived with Annie, the musical director and my PA at the City Hall at eight o'clock on the day of the auditions, in plenty of time to prepare - as we thought. As we turned the corner we were faced with an astonishing sight. The auditions were not due to start for another two and a half hours, but a long queue of children and parents had formed already. They were all beaming with excitement and optimism despite the cold, damp weather. Many of them were running through the words of *Matchstalk Men* ready for the audition.

I asked the doorkeeper if he would let them in out of the cold, but he shook his head. It was a council building – rules and regulations and all that.

By the time Marti arrived at nine, the City Hall was encircled by a queue three deep.

"You see why we wouldn't let them in early" said the doorman, smugly.

"Some of them might be back home again by now if you had" I countered.

The TV crews had arrived and were interviewing the children about their dreams of fame with Marti. Apparently Trevor Macdonald was coming down with a team from ITN. Overhead, the Yorkshire Television helicopter was circling, while the *Sun* and the *Daily Mirror* had photographers combing the line for perspective stars. I hadn't expected anything like this.

"If we're going to audition them all I'll have to cancel my winter break" said Marti. I promised her we would do most of the work, but that wasn't how she saw things.

"Don't worry, I'm staying here till we've seen the last one" she said. "It's me up there on stage with them - I want to make sure we have the right kids."

She was right, of course. She smiled at me and gave me another hug - a public act of support which I very much appreciated.

The Daily News reporter told us that sales of *Matchstalk Men and Matchstalk Cats and Dogs* from the Yorkshire area alone had kept the song in the charts for another week. We all wondered how on earth we were going to sit through a thousand renditions of it.

We started dead on time at 10.30 and we were still there at 10.30 that night. We even had to come back the following day, when the theatre was again crammed with young hopefuls. They were now coming from Nottingham, Leicester, Manchester as well as Sheffield. It was a terrific public relations success, but we were all far too tired to congratulate ourselves.

That weekend we were in most of the Sunday papers. Marti was interviewed on the BBC's *Breakfast Time* to tell the world what all the fuss was about. The City Hall opened an advance booking office to cope with the demand for tickets.

With great difficulty, we managed to choose our 40 children. They were a mixed bunch, which of course was what we wanted. They ranged from a Vietnamese boat child of eight to a ten-year-old Sheffield lad who was in care and had to walk to the audition as he couldn't afford the bus fare. The boy had never stepped on a stage before, but Marti took to him immediately and that night she took him back to his care home. Next morning, visibly upset, she told me she had found the house boarded up, and though his mother was there she had been the worse for drink. He had had to scramble through a side window to get in.

There were some lovely dancers and many good singing voices, along with some unique personalities. While many of the children had never stepped on to a stage before, some were old hands at it. Our job was to get the two to blend, and Judith Sylvester proved a miracle worker in that department.

Chapter 11

The rehearsals went well. We had to replace only one child, and that was for medical reasons. Judith was very strict. The children held her in deep respect and they all responded one hundred per cent to all she asked of them.

Naturally all the children fell in love with Marti, and she with them. It was a very happy time.

The routines were established in the first month and polished over the next two. "You must know it backwards" Marti would tell them. "In a circus, the clown can't be funny on the tightrope until he has really mastered it. Only when he can walk it properly with no effort can he start being funny."

At the end of the seventh week we put the rehearsal piano away and in came the seventeen- piece orchestra. The children had never heard anything like it.

The opening night was tremendous. The people of Sheffield had never seen a group of children like it, so talented, so professional. As Marti chatted, joked, danced and sang her way through the concert, she was lifted to great heights by these extraordinary children. The show lived up to its title. That night Sheffield let Marti know in no uncertain way that she did indeed belong to them.

Much praise was showered on Annie for her costumes. The children looked spectacular at every entrance. Annie loved making and dressing Marti - she found her tall, slender figure a dream to dress.

"She really works her clothes" said Annie. "She's fussy but she knows what's right for her." Annie went on to make more clothes for Marti after the show finished, and they became good friends.

The press went crazy. We didn't get a single bad review. The tabloids did full-page pullouts with glowing reviews, for the whole five weeks. Almost every child had his or her turn in the spotlight. Marti Caine said she had never had such fantastic notices. There were quite a few celebrities in the audience – Rolf Harris, Tommy Steele and Des O'Connor joined us. On most nights the 'SOLD OUT' boards had to be brought out.

The council asked if I would agree to do it again the following Christmas, but I said no - the show was, after all, *'Once In A Lifetime'*. We knew that second time around it could not possibly be the same.

I did tour the show briefly after the run finished, to Torquay at the Princess Theatre with Lionel Blair and children, to Southport with Billy Dainty, to Blackpool with the Blue Peter team, and to Paignton with Lorraine Chase. It did well everywhere. Then at the end of the year I put it all to bed.

A very special reward came some years later when I was invited along with Annie to a series of West End shows, including *Cats, 42nd Street, Phantom of the Opera, The Royal Variety Show and Les Miserables*. Quite a few of my lovely Sheffield children had parts in these shows, and it was wonderful to see them growing up and tackling such difficult work.

One of the boys became one of the stars of the TV series *Casualty,* and was quite a pin-up among the girls. I was flattered when the BBC put together their own format with *Kids International*, but to my mind these children did not have the lovely raw edge our Sheffield kids had. They were hand-picked from the best London stage schools, unlike our kids, who had walked in off the street and gone straight in at the deep end.

Fifteen years after *Once In A Lifetime*, Marti died of lymphatic cancer at the age of 51. Her friends knew it was coming – she had fought the illness for some time – but it was still a dreadful loss to all who knew her. She dealt with her illness with humour and sensitivity and spent her last years campaigning tirelessly for cancer charities. The reassurance she gave her fellow patients at Weston Park Hospital in Sheffield was extraordinary.

Chapter 11

Marti was the finest ambassador for courage. 'Love's last gift is remembrance.'

The funeral was at Sheffield Cathedral, a stone's throw away from the City Hall. As the coffin was carried into the cathedral, the trams, buses and taxis all stopped, and the crowds in the streets bowed their heads in silence. The pews were full of household names who had come to pay their respects, as well as many of the children whom she had brought into the world of entertainment.

Marti produced her own funeral. She had recorded some songs as her way of saying goodbye, and had asked her accompanist to play her favourite pieces. She had also recorded a short speech, which was played to us over the PA system. To hear her talking to us again like that in the cathedral was quite shattering.

As the coffin was carried out, I listened to the sobbing and realised how extraordinarily popular she had been and how much she had meant to so many people. As the Mayor of Sheffield said, "We have lost a true daughter of Yorkshire".

Marti Caine left a legacy of love. She devoted a great deal of time to working with children with special needs and today many hundreds of these children are still benefiting from her inexhaustible efforts.

Some of the children who starred in *Once In A Lifetime* now bring their own children to see Annie and me. We all sit around chatting and reminiscing about those days, and reflecting what we would give to have Marti there with us.

Chapter 12

A show for Simon

After the Sheffield show, Brian and Michael sent me a copy of their album. All the songs were based on Lowry's paintings, portraying life in the mills and the hard world of the industrial North West. Frankly, I never wanted to hear *Matchstalk Men and Matchstalk Cats and Dogs* again, but the collection of songs gave me an idea – a musical based on the world Lowry had painted.

Lowry, The Concert recreated the Manchester of old with its mills, the weavers and the clattering of the looms. It was all carefully researched and reproduced, and we received much praise for the originality of the concept and the music. Brian and Michael headed a talented cast of actors and dancers who had all the right ingredients. The show became something of a cult, and its educational flavour gave it strong appeal to schools and universities.

The public at large, however, did not turn out in great numbers. Modern audiences want colourful shows with big names, and we failed to pull in the crowds. A single hit, I learned, was not enough to guarantee a good box office.

This was my first lesson as a producer – don't let your heart rule your head. With the profit I had made from *Once In A Lifetime* rapidly disappearing, I called time on the show. Yet I never regretted *Lowry, The Concert*. It was such good fun – and it led indirectly to something more rewarding.

It happened in Peterborough, where we putting Lowry on for a week at the Key Theatre. They had left a copy of that day's *Sunday Express* in my hotel room, and the lead story and photo caught my eye. The story was about a nine-year-old boy called Simon Bostock, who it seemed would die if he couldn't be given an urgent bone marrow transplant. On top of this, I read that Simon's mother had killed herself because of her own terminal illness, while his father was suffering from cancer and was close to the end himself. I was appalled – it would be hard to imagine a family in a worse situation.

That story kept nagging at me. It just wouldn't go away. The look on that little boy's face! I had a healthy son nearly the same age as Simon, yet we lucky old Stirlings were all in good health and enjoying life to the full. It all seemed so unfair.

I picked up the phone and telephoned the newsdesk at the Sunday Express. Luck was on my side – the editor, Derek Jameson, was in that night and was taking calls about Simon personally.

I asked Derek if I could be of any help. He said he had already set up a Simon Bostock Fund to pay for the bone marrow operation the boy so desperately needed at Great Ormond Street children's hospital. I explained that I was in a position to put on a concert in the West End to raise money for the fund.

"Can you really do that?" Derek asked. "Forgive me for being blunt, but a lot of people have offered in good faith to help Simon. When it comes down to it they very often can't deliver."

I told him I could definitely put on a show, if he would agree. I promised to come back to him with a proposal.

I started the process there and then in my hotel room. I rang a contact of mine, Michael Rosenberg, an associate of David Frost at his company David Paradine Ltd. Michael had seen the article and understood what I was talking about.

I knew Michael was known to sympathise with such causes and had a strong desire to help youngsters in trouble. He also ran a media company, so he understood the ins and outs of the press and television. He had great financial expertise, and always seemed to know the right person for the right job.

Michael told me to go ahead with the production side of things. He even offered to guarantee the costs of the evening, if he wasn't able to secure help from others. He promised to approach friends and business colleagues with a view to raising sponsorship and revenue for this deserving cause. Michael said that it was important to him that all the money we raised should go to help Simon.

I told him I wanted the show to go ahead in a fortnight, while the story was still fresh in everybody's minds. Michael was concerned that I had set myself an impossible task, but I assured him he need have no worries on that score.

I booked the Theatre Royal in Drury Lane for the show. Michael provided an apartment overlooking Hyde Park, complete with two secretaries and everything I needed to get the show underway. It was handy to be right in the middle of London and within walking distance of most of the people I needed to talk to.

Derek Jameson and the *Sunday Express* team were very supportive. They gave me daily coverage in the paper, and each time I persuaded another star to appear they would publish a story and photo. Headlines like *Stars Come Out For Simon* helped to make the show a more attractive proposition.

Chapter 12

Advance bookings started to pour in. It was all looking very healthy. There's no-one like the great British public for coming to the rescue when you need them.

Theatre people are marvellous when it comes to helping good causes. They'll move mountains if they have to, very often without expecting much credit. Artists' private time is precious to them, yet they will give it up to help others and to use their names and their faces to support a good cause.

One day a call came through from Danny La Rue, who was appearing in his summer show in Scarborough. Danny had an extraordinary plan. He would hire a coach for the Saturday, throw his entire company on board, musicians and all, and drive through the night to take part in my show on the Sunday.

I told Danny I didn't know how to thank him.

"I don't want thanks, love, I want this father and son to have some sort of chance" he said.

I had my top of the bill! Danny was a very big star, with a huge following in London.

Within three days of the news that we were getting Danny, we had sold half the 3000 tickets to *Simon's Show*. Danny's involvement quickly prompted other artists to join the show. Before long we had Ronnie Corbett, Dennis Waterman and his band and the principals of the Royal Ballet at Convent Garden, with Darcey Bussell. Esther Rantzen offered to host the night. Anthony Andrews, Wayne Sleep and his dancers, Robert Powell, Richard Beckinsale, Paula Wilcox, Richard O'Sullivan... I couldn't believe all these household names were willing to do our show.

I put together an extract from *Lowry the Concert* with Brian and Michael and featuring the Blue Peter team, who had already raised a considerable sum for Simon through their TV show.

The icing on the cake was a special appearance by Morecambe and Wise. It could not be publicised at first, as the boys were not sure if the TV company would let them off, but the green light came soon enough. Ten days after announcing the show, I had a cast of 100. In fact the show was if anything looking rather on the long side – but on the night, the audience didn't mind seeing so many stars having fun together.

I will never forget taking Simon Bostock backstage to meet Danny. The look on the boy's face when he saw this statuesque 'woman' with his make-up, flashing earrings, sequins and wig, all in strange contrast to the deep voice, was a sight to behold.

"Hello young Simon" said Danny. "I've been looking forward to meeting you."

Simon was struck dumb. He just tucked his head under his dad's arm.

Soon he was persuaded to sit on Danny's knee in front of the dressing-room mirror as the star put the finishing touches to his makeup. He was enthralled by the mirror with all its bright lamps lit up around him. He had a fit of the giggles when Danny tried a couple of his wigs on him and his father.

Danny then presented Simon with a present from Hamleys' toy shop - a spectacular train set. Danny had had it specially delivered. Simon's eyes lit up.

Danny La Rue paid for that coach, he paid his dancers, his musicians and his wardrobe and wig staff so that he could do that show for that little boy. No wonder the audience rose to the occasion.

Dennis Waterman proved that he was an accomplished singer as well as an actor by performing a great set with his country and western band. The Royal Ballet sequence with principals and full chorus was beautiful, and Wayne Sleep and his dancers were great fun.

Derek Jameson was thrilled with it all – both with the show, which he and his wife watched with Simon and his father from the Royal Box, and more importantly with the money we raised. It was enough give the Simon Bostock Bone Marrow Fund a great start.

The artists insisted that some of the money should be used to pay for Simon and his father to take a long holiday in Malta. It would give them time to bond again as father and son and adjust to what was happening, out of the glare of publicity.

Of course, we could not help Simon's mum. We all wished we had been able to do our bit just a little bit earlier to save her from what she went through. It might have given her the courage and support to carry on.

Neither could our efforts alleviate Simon's dad's anguish as his own condition steadily worsened. But we all lived in hope that Simon himself would benefit from the knowledge of how much we cared. And we had made public the needs of the many other children like him with bone marrow conditions.

Since that time there have been remarkable medical advances in treatment and many young lives have been transformed. That stands as a small reward to those of us who took part in that show.

Michael Rosenberg and David Frost were delighted with the outcome and offered to take on more such ventures, should the need arise. Later the following year we took them up on their offer by presenting another show at the Theatre Royal, *To Tina With Love*, for a young Downs Syndrome girl who wanted to help her friends. This too was a great success.

Chapter 12

I stayed in the Hyde Park flat for two weeks after *Simon's Show* to help the Grade Organisation with a variety bill at The London Palladium starring two American stars, Eddie Fisher and Lorna Luft.

Then Blue Peter contacted me to say that they wanted to do another programme on Lowry. Would I put together a piece with children in clogs, cloth caps, and shawls with Brian and Michael?

I was delighted to take on this challenge, and the experience became a valuable lesson to me. Theatre and television are very different media. The Blue Peter special was a huge success and the programme got one of its highest ratings with its 'Lowry' production.

The Drury Lane audience gave our short extract of *Lowry* a standing ovation. The crowd clapped and stamped along with the three big production numbers. In fact, the theatre manager was showing concern that the excessive stamping in the circles might cause some damage!

A lesson for producers - it doesn't matter how 'good' your show is – all that matters is whether it works. Countless producers have lost their socks by clinging on to an unjustified belief in a show and keeping it going for too long, hoping that the tide will turn and the crowds will start turning up. This very rarely happens. We cannot make the public attend - they have to want to see the production.

Gert and Daisy

Working with children was a revelation, as well as a very happy experience. However, it did have one drawback - their mothers.

I always did my best to avoid any sort of confrontation, but inevitably there were a few times when someone's mum would decide to take me and the whole system on single-handedly, because little Tracey or darling Dominic was not given the starring role they so clearly had been born to play.

During the years when I was doing shows with children I encountered a remarkable assortment of mothers, from the decent ones who had nothing but their children's best interests at heart to the hardline matriarchs who were determined to get their little ones to the top any way they could.

Some of the things that happened backstage would probably have landed me in court if I hadn't been careful. You wouldn't believe the antics some stage mothers put me through. In the end, instead of just recounting the incidents to friends and colleagues, I decided to write a musical on the subject.

The show was called *Cheers Mrs Worthington*, a reference to the famous Noël Coward song *Don't Put Your Daughter On The Stage, Mrs Worthington*. The play was based on my own experiences with stage mothers. I set it in three acts, dealing with three different encounters. The score and songs were written by the talented Grahame Maclean.

Chapter 13

Act 1 featured a woman who had dabbled in show business herself in her younger years, but had never achieved glory, principally because she had no talent. She had a very attractive daughter who was making a considerable impact on the music scene and forging ahead as her mother had only dreamed of doing.

This woman wanted to control her daughter's career, but the daughter sensibly had other ideas. Mum managed, however, to demolish her daughter's chances at every turn, so that in the end neither of them achieved their ambitions.

Diana Coupland played the mother, with the very bright Catrina Hillton-Hull as the daughter. Charlie Drake played the musical director, using his comic ability to the full as he tried valiantly to conduct the orchestra while this wreck of a mother kept telling him it was all at the wrong tempo. The two stars made the audiences laugh and cry practically simultaneously.

In Act 2 we saw a mother dragging her henpecked husband around as their daughter auditioned for anything and everything that was going, regardless of whether she was remotely suitable for the part. The father, played by Charlie, wasn't allowed to utter a word. Charlie loved this part as there were no lines to learn, and with every sideways glance he brought the house down. The daughter, who actually wanted to be an athlete, was played by Suzanne Dando, who in real life had achieved great prowess in the Olympics for her country.

Act 3 showed a songwriter trying to find a young and attractive female singer to partner him in the Eurovision song contest. He finds just the girl he's looking for - played by Diane Lee, one half of the singing due Peters & Lee. Then - enter the dragon. Mother immediately wants the lyrics rewritten to suit her daughter, arguing about the contract and the percentage her daughter will be receiving. The song is not good enough and neither is the money, she says. Mum insists on choosing her daughter's clothes, appointing a press agent, even inserting a non-marriage clause.

The boy decides he has no choice but to go it alone. He goes on to win the *Eurovision Song Contest* and reaches great heights worldwide, leaving the mother to face her daughter in a very poignant last song.

Some of the songs were hits in their own right, and *Cheers Mrs Worthington*, the title song, was recorded by Kenny Baker and his jazz band. The show toured for nine weeks with mixed reviews, but Charlie Drake never failed to bring the house down every night.

My next production became the favourite of my career, and gave me enormous pleasure. I had always been a great fan of variety, and one Sunday I went to Llandudno, to take in a show along the pier and look out for new talent.

Before the show began I went for a walk around the town and looked in the window of an antiques shop. It had an extensive collection of old theatre posters for sale, mainly highlighting shows of bygone eras that had been presented in the town. Among this bunch of memorabilia was a poster advertising a pre-war concert starring Elsie and Doris Waters, better known on stage as Gert and Daisy.

The poster took my fancy, so I bought it and slipped it into my briefcase. I remembered Elsie and Doris Waters well, not least because I had worked for many years as a child actor with their brother, Jack Warner of *Dixon of Dock Green* fame. I also remembered them for their radio shows, with their naughty ditties and little sketches over the garden fence.

When I got home I started to research these two ladies in detail. I sat for hours in the BBC's archives listening to *Henry Hall's Guest Nights* and *Variety Bandbox* - wonderfully funny radio shows of an earlier era.

Chapter 13

It seemed Elsie Waters, though much the older of the pair, was still with us. She was now in her nineties and living in a bungalow in West Byfleet, Sussex. I wrote to Elsie, saying how much I would love to meet her. I got an immediate response in the shape of a lovely notelet inviting me to West Byfleet for afternoon tea.

I was greeted at the front porch by a very tall, elegantly attired lady wearing upmarket country clothing. Elsie was six feet tall and slim with it. She stood very straight for her years and was quite obviously well in control. She was witty, charming and very entertaining, with a sharp brain and a dignified manner in keeping with her status as one of the queens of light entertainment.

I was ushered into the drawing room of her bungalow. There was a grand piano in the corner which bore many signed, framed photographs. I spotted the Queen Mother and Noël Coward among them. She noticed me trying to read the message the Queen Mother had written. "We sat together at Her Majesty's sewing circles" she explained.

Elsie settled into her sofa, facing a large window with a breathtaking panorama of the Sussex countryside.

"Pretty, isn't it" she said, looking at the view. "Doris loved this time of the day, tea with little sandwiches, no crusts, her favourites."

Elsie made tea for us and served it on a silver tray. Then she nestled into one end of the sofa. She seemed to have left a lot of space at the other, almost as if someone else was occupying it. I noticed that although the other end was empty, it featured a very pronounced dip.

It dawned on me that of course the dip had been left by Doris, who had died seven years before, and it was not going to be disturbed by anyone else. Elsie was insistent that the memory of her beloved Doris must be fully respected, a request to which I was very happy to agree.

Elsie proved to be an extremely interesting lady, and very amusing. Despite her age, her wit was entirely contemporary - there was no harking back to the 'good old days' as I'd half expected.

It was remarkable to discover how very different these two sophisticated sisters had been from their stage personalities. Gert and Daisy were working-class Cockney neighbours saddled with lazy, unseen husbands, Bert and Wally. They would appear on stage in old cardigans held together by safety pins, cloche hats which seemed cemented to their heads, old support stockings, pinafores and overalls. The chat could be naughty and there were frequent innuendoes, 'to keep the lads happy', as Elsie put it. In real life the sisters lived very comfortably, eating at the best restaurants and travelling everywhere in their chauffeur-driven Bentley.

Elsie told me her story - and what a story it was. She and her sister had toured the best variety theatres, giving hundreds of radio broadcasts, making films, guesting at many important dinners and evenings. They had entertained the troops in Europe, and even in Burma, despite the dangers.

In the train on the way home, I puzzled over what I could do with my discovery. Eventually I came up with a plan.

I spent the following four months writing a musical about the sisters called - what else? - *Gert and Daisy*. Elsie had given me so much material that it took quite a while to collate it all. She sent me transcripts of their radio shows and books containing their songs and ditties. What was extraordinary was how much she trusted me.

I was particularly pleased with a scene depicting Gert and Daisy in Burma. It was based on an incident in which a critically-injured soldier had been carried into camp on a stretcher. He was not expected to live through the night.

Elsie and Doris took one side of the stretcher each and held his hands. They recreated some of their sketches for him and sang a selection of songs. The soldier's grip got tighter and tighter on their hands as he faded away. The scene had a tremendous impact on the audience and was mentioned over and over again in the reviews.

Elsie sent me one of her lovely notelets: "Dear John, please do me an enormous favour and make sure Vera Lynn sees these reviews - even better, that she goes to see the show!"

I took Annie with me to see Elsie's wardrobes. Elsie opened the doors to reveal racks of Norman Hartnell gowns, dresses and sequinned tops, all mothballed and in order. The two sides of the wardrobe were identical, with arrays of court shoes all in shoe bags, hats, boas, the lot. There must have been forty sets of evening attire on each side.

Annie's eyes popped out of her head, as it would be her job to recreate all these wonderful clothes. Fortunately, Elsie was prepared to lend a selection of them to her for her to copy.

Now to find actresses who could play these two famous sisters. This was going to a real challenge.

I was always very clear who I wanted to play Doris - Rosemary Leach. Rosemary had just finished an award-winning run in the West End, in *84 Charing Cross Road*. She was at the top of her career, with a heavy forthcoming schedule and television and films. My only chance, as I saw it, was to ask her to accompany me to Byfleet to meet Elsie for tea.

The pair got on like a house on fire. There was a good deal of laughter that afternoon. By the time we left, Rosemary was on board.

Chapter 13

Finding someone for Elsie was more difficult. I took several big female names down to Byfleet - very talented artists like Geraldine McEwan and Jill Gascoigne - but for one reason or another Elsie was not comfortable with any of them.

I hit the jackpot with Sylvia Syms, one of the finest film actresses of the day. Elsie was very happy for Sylvia to play her, and gave her the same warm reception she had with Rosemary.

The most talented impressionist in the country at that time was Peter Goodwright, who could play just about anyone. He specialised in radio stars past and present. One man to play 50 parts, I thought - he could do Winston Churchill as easily as Henry Hall.

When I took Rosemary and Sylvia to meet Peter they were very much taken by this gentle and lovable man. Unsurprisingly Peter was somewhat daunted by the challenge, but he was game to try it. Elsie adored Peter, particularly when he started doing his impressions of the stars she had known so well.

Terry Wogan asked if he could devote one of his TV chat shows to the musical and invited Elsie to join him on his sofa for a chat about it all. Terry told me later that it had been one of the most enjoyable shows he had done, and well as one of the most watched. I will always remember the opening of the TV show, when Peter turned round to face the audience with his orchestra behind him and uttered those magical words. "Good Evening Ladies and Gentlemen, I'm Henry Hall and this is my guest night."

I toured *Gert and Daisy* for eight weeks to get it in shape for the West End. The availability of theatres was a problem. We needed an intimate theatre like the Fortune, the Ambassador's or maybe Wyndhams. We decided to wait for the Fortune, which would shortly become free. Unfortunately for us Sylvia Syms was then asked to make an important film, and as I could not promise her a date yet for the West End I had no option but to let her go at the end of the tour.

The Thorndike theatre in Leatherhead asked me if I would do a limited season with *Gert and Daisy* to hold it together while we lined up the London theatres. Rosemary and Peter were agreeable but I had to find a new Elsie - with just ten days to reopening.

To my delight, the comedy actress Josephine Tewson jumped into the part. Her talent for comic timing added a new dimension to the show and Rosemary and Josephine became friends on and off the stage. Josephine gave a different slant to the part of Elsie, but Elsie was very happy with this and thought she brought a refreshing difference to the production.

Privately however, things were not going well. I was finding it difficult to keep my financial backers happy, and money was getting worryingly tight. It was hard to keep the show going after Leatherhead. In the end I had no choice but to close it.

I was sad that this piece of history never had the airing in the West End it deserved. I was sorry for Annie too, as she had made such an impact with the costumes.

I was now in serious trouble financially, and praying for a break. We had had to move from our Brighton home into a small flat to try and keep costs down.

Then Alan Boyd, Head of Light Entertainment at London Weekend Television, heard through the grapevine that I was in a spot of bother. He asked me if I would join the production team at LWT as talent coordinator, as their man had just left to go to ATV. It would only be a 12-month contract to start with, but that was fine by me.

We moved into a bedsit on Brighton seafront, not far from Hove, where

Chapter 13

my mother and Claude were living. There were only two of us now - Mark had moved back to Manchester to take on a new job in lighting. He was working on big conferences both in this country and abroad, and having a great time. So Annie and I felt we could survive better by living simply for a while. for me it was back to television, and for Annie it was back to the sewing room.

Chapter 14

Divine intervention

Annie was now yearning for a career change. She needed a break from the daily demands of the theatre, and a rest from the dark and dusty costume departments where she had slaved for so many long hours.

She decided to set up in business making wedding dresses - and for that we would need a shop. We found one in the village of Hurstpierpoint, about six miles from Brighton. It had been a tailor's shop, and was just what Annie had in mind.

Hurstpierpoint was a revelation in more ways than one. It had a medieval look to it, with its Tudor half-timbered shopfronts overhanging the high street.

We moved Annie into the shop and started trying to get the locals interested. We promoted her originality and creativity, and plugged the advantages of having your clothes hand-made and designed for you. The village embraced her expertise and welcomed her into the fold, alongside the art shop, the jeweller's, the fishmonger, the vegetable wholesaler, the café and the butcher.

It was astonishing to see how these shops did business with each other. Annie soon got dragged into the 'bartering and favours co-operative' run by the other shopkeepers. I have never seen such a strong sense of community.

For example, I had needed to have my front teeth crowned for some time but had never got around to it - not least because of the cost. The shop next door had a dental surgery above it. Annie got a visit from one of the dentists one day asking if she could make him a morning suit for his daughter's impending wedding in South Africa.

She agreed, and the dentist asked her if there was anything he could do in return, under the village favour scheme. She asked if he might do my crowns for me. The deal was done, he got a superb suit and I got a splendid job done on my teeth. We both looked much smarter for the deal, and neither of us had had to put our hands in our pockets.

Then the fishmonger asked Annie if she could make her a couple of dresses and skirts, as she could never find anything to fit properly. For this favour she would supply Annie for the next couple of months with fish for our table. We got top-quality salmon, cod, halibut, Dover sole - all sorts, for the next two months. We ate well, and the fishmonger was the best dressed in the village.

A month later the greengrocer's daughter was to be married and both she and her daughter needed kitting out... you can guess the rest. We needed no groceries for the year ahead. I don't believe during our stay at Hurstpierpoint anyone ever put their hands in their pocket for anything.

It was all very civilised, but in the end the shop did not fulfil Annie's dreams. The monotony of having to be there every day and at all hours didn't suit her. So we said a sad farewell to our new friends, shut up shop and moved back to the north.

I began travelling round the UK and Europe to look for talent for London Weekend TV. I was attached to shows like the *Royal Variety Show, Game for a Laugh* and *Surprise, Surprise*. LWT were very strong on light entertainment and they were using up acts faster than I could find them, but it was all good fun.

Chapter 14

At the end of my contract at The Pink Palace, as the LWT HQ was named - it had been built by a Middle Eastern consortium and fitted out very opulently - I had done more than 50 shows. It was then that I got a call from the BBC.

Peter Rysdale Scott was in charge of the Manchester BBC drama department. He was looking for a project for my old friend Patricia Hayes. Patricia was by now one of our leading character actresses and much sought after. He wanted to follow up her tremendous success in 1971 with her television play *Edna the Inebriate Woman*, in which she depicted a homeless alcoholic who caused trouble and mayhem everywhere and would not accept help from anyone.

This was a very serious and poignant piece of writing by Jeremy Sandford, who had also written *Cathy Come Home,* and it had a tremendous impact. Patricia won many awards for her performance. She had researched the part by living as a vagrant, visiting soup kitchens and staying on the streets with other less fortunate beings. After filming *Edna* she became involved with *Shelter,* the organisation which looks after homeless people.

While the BBC were anxious to keep Patricia, the independent companies were working hard to win her over and had come up with several tempting ideas for her to consider. But she had spent a lifetime with the BBC and she wanted to stay with the Corporation.

Patricia had jokingly mentioned to me how annoyed she had been not to have qualified for the part of Elsie Waters. She would have been wonderful in the role, except that she wasn't much more than half Elsie's height. So she asked Peter Rysdale Scott if I could come up with something original for her, preferably in a rather lighter vein than *Edna*. Understandably, she didn't want to put herself through all that trauma again.

After six weeks of working day and night non-stop I came up with a 90-

minute play for Patricia called *Marked for Life*. It was the story of an elderly recluse called Rachel who lived alone in a dilapidated farmhouse overlooking a fishing village in South Devon. She kept a dozen donkeys, all named after the apostles - Luke, Matthew, John, Simon, Thaddeus and so on.

A twelve-year-old boy called Anthony had arrived in the village with his mother, who had taken on the housekeeper's job at a local hotel. He loved to visit the donkeys, but Rachel would chase him away as she had no time for intruders.

When one of the donkeys became ill, Rachel caught the boy with him and sent him packing. But the vet, who had struggled in vain to cure the animal with medication, noticed an improvement after the boy's visit and tried to make Rachel relent a little. Gradually she began to see him with new eyes. She was acutely aware of the biblical significance of donkeys, whose characteristic cross markings are said to have been put there by Jesus Christ, and began to view the boy's arrival as divine intervention.

The BBC loved it, and so did Pat. It was a little on the serious side, but a good deal lighter than Edna. The fact that Pat happened to love donkeys helped greatly.

For research purposes the BBC sent me off one Friday to Chelford, in Cheshire, where there was a monthly horse auction. They had been told some donkeys were arriving there from Ireland that day. I asked Annie to come with me - a decision which, as it turned out, would change both our lives.

We walked slowly round the pens surveying the assortment of animals which were going on sale. There were carthorses destined for the French meat market and ponies of all shapes and sizes which were no longer wanted by their owners. And right at the end of the warehouse, in a corner

Chapter 14

all alone, we found what we were looking for - two forlorn little donkeys.

The animals were both very much the worse for wear, and appeared terrified and in shock from their long journey without food or water. They were thrusting their muzzles against the back wall, trying to blot out the noise and confusion.

Annie gasped in horror. She was moved to tears.

"What can we do?" she sobbed.

"Nothing" I said. I couldn't see how we could help these poor beasts in any way.

We asked at the reception area what was going to happen to the animals. A charmless woman explained, very matter-of-factly, that they would come up for auction at the end of the day. If they failed to reach their sale price, they would go straight to the pet food market.

I looked at Annie. "Do you want me to take you home?" I put my arm round her, trying to console her.

"Not without the donkeys" she said.

"Come on, we can't possibly buy them! Where would we put them?"

"We'll find somewhere."

Annie was very upset, and very determined. She told the woman about the injuries, the lice, and the scars we could see on the donkeys, but she might as well have been talking to the wall. Clearly, for a horse market, this was all quite normal.

We waited for a couple of hours while the horses and ponies all went through the auction. Annie stayed with the two donkeys until it was their turn. Neither of us had ever been in an auction ring, so we had no idea what to expect.

Chapter 14

At last our two poor donkeys were driven into the ring. They stood pathetically in the centre, terrified and alone. The man who was selling them hit them a couple of times to demonstrate that they could walk. He tried to make them do a circuit of the perimeter wall, but they were having none of it. One had its head firmly wedged on to the other's back.

I noticed that one of the animals was grey, while the other was brown. They both had thick black crosses across their shoulders, which made me think of my play for Patricia and the religious significance of these appealing little beasts of burden.

The bidding started at £20. An arm went up - £30. A wink from another corner and it was £40. Then £50.

Annie dug me sharply in the ribs. "Put your arm up!" she hissed.

I raised my arm, and Annie shouted "Fifty-five pounds!"

"Just a hand will do sir," said the auctioneer.

Someone tipped a flat cap - £60.

"Offer him a hundred!" Annie shouted at me, desperate now not to lose her donkeys.

"Are you sure?"

"Do it, NOW!" .

I cleared my throat. "One hundred pounds" I quavered.

"A hundred it is" said the auctioneer, dropping his gavel "That's guineas, Mister...?"

"Stirling" I whispered.

"Guineas, Mr Stirling, is that all right?" "Yes."

Chapter 14

"One hundred guineas to Mr Stirling, sold." Down went the hammer.

"Just pay at reception please Mr Stirling, we'll have them ready for you at the door" said the auctioneer.

I was in shock. Where on earth were we going to put two donkeys? How were we going to get them home in the first place?

Annie was already cuddling her new charges and telling them that there was nothing to worry about any more. Not for them perhaps, I thought. She had already christened the grey one Baz and was racking her brains for a name for the other.

So began a new chapter in our lives together. Out of the blue, the safety curtain had come down on the life we had known. Gone were the costumes, the dancing girls, the bands, the bouquets and the curtain calls. Baz and Danny, as we eventually named our brown donkey, had given us a new beginning. It was our turn to be 'marked for life'.

Chapter 15

Donkey business

There are times in everybody's life when you need a really good friend. As I stood in the car park wondering what on earth we were going to do with our two battered little refugees, it occurred to me that this was most definitely one of them.

I could think of just one person who might be able to help - Keith Hopwood, who had once been the lead guitarist in a pop group called Herman's Hermits. Keith had written many of their hits, and we had later worked together in Great Yarmouth. We had got on well and kept in touch ever since.

I now remembered that Keith had moved to Tarporley in Cheshire, only half an hour's drive away from Chelford. He and his wife Maria had bought a lovely old manor house called Hullgrave Hall. Keith had moved his recording business from Manchester to a new 24-track recording studio in the grounds.

I phoned Keith and explained the situation we were in. He laughed at the image of me standing with two donkeys in the middle of nowhere, but as I explained the animals' plight he listened attentively. When I'd finished speaking he didn't hesitate. Yes of course - the donkeys would be welcome at Hullgrave Hall. They might even give him inspiration. He was now busy writing music for films and TV programmes, particularly for children's productions, from Roahl Dahl films to *Bob the Builder*.

126

Chapter 15

This came as a huge relief. I went over to a waiting horsebox driver who was touting for business and explained where we were wanted to take our donkeys. He quoted me £100 in cash for the trip.

I noticed there were already three horses in the back of the horsebox, so I asked him if he could section the horses off. I explained that my donkeys were very weak. He wasn't impressed by this request.

"I know what I'm doing son, I do this for a living" he growled.

"They've been through a lot today, can't we please try and make the journey comfortable for them?" I pleaded.

"They're only donkeys" he said, smiling patronisingly at Annie, who did not smile back. In fact she looked as if she was about to knee him in a place where he would remember it for a very long time.

"You get the cash and I'll get the donkeys to where you want them in one piece and that's that" he said. "Don't give me any claptrap about being comfortable, I've been doing this for too long. If you're not happy with it you can walk them to your fancy friend's house on foot." I could see he meant it.

It occurred to me that this man would be useful for my play. I could include a scene in which Pat tore him off a strip for his cruelty to donkeys. A sweet revenge!

I still had my pad and pencil in my coat pocket, so I quietly made a few notes - the elbow patches, the baling twine round the man's waist, his lank and greasy mop of hair. To this fellow, donkeys were nothing more than pieces of meat. He watched me scribbling with puzzled eyes, then started to get the ramp down.

I then had to pay a visit to the mobile equine shop to buy some collars and ropes, without which taking the donkeys anywhere at all would have been impossible. I ended up buying horsefeed and feeding buckets, coats (the nights were cold), polo mints and ginger nut biscuits. It took me two trips to carry it all back. The cheapest part of this increasingly costly day had been the donkeys themselves.

Putting the head collars on proved a stressful business, both for us and the poor donkeys, who could sense our nerves and our inability to cope. Then we had to try to persuade the donkeys to walk to the horsebox. No matter how we tried to coax them, they were determined to stay exactly where they were.

The driver had a satisfied smirk on his face. These sentimental townies were learning the facts of life about handling donkeys - the hard way.

"Give me that bucket" he sneered, after watching us for a while. "Now put some feed in it, they'll soon shift."

We did as instructed. The donkeys took no notice whatsoever.

"Right" he said, gesturing at Baz. "Get the rope round the donkey's arse and one of you grab each end of the rope. When I say pull, pull."

This, surely, would work. But it was of no use. Neither Baz nor Danny would budge an inch.

The driver was beginning to lose his temper. If Annie hadn't been there I feel sure he would have started taking it out on the poor animals with his stick. But there was £100 at stake, and it was as much in the driver's interests as ours to get the animals moving.

Finally he called over a group of his colleagues, six large and intimidating men. Between them they dragged the donkeys to the lorry and up the ramp. But the two beasts took one look at the ramp leading up into the lorry, and planted their hooves again.

Chapter 15

The driver was now fuming.

"Right" he said. "Tell your wife to go and have a cup of tea while we'll deal with this."

Annie wasn't having that. She stayed put.

In the end a group of the men simply picked Baz up like a chest of drawers, carried him into the van and plonked him down. The other donkey was so frightened at this - or so anxious not to be left on his own - that he bolted straight up the ramp and joined him.

By the time we got to Tarporley, Keith and Maria had prepared one of the stables with shavings, hay and straw and a brimming bucket of water. I was impressed, and deeply grateful. The two donkeys came down the ramp and went straight into the paddock. It wasn't long before they were both rolling contentedly in the first clean, fresh bedding they had seen for a long time. All I had to do now was find them a permanent home.

The Peak District had become very special to us. In the year since I had written Pat's play we had sold our little flat in Brighton for an excellent price and bought a far more spacious two-storey apartment in Buxton, opposite the cricket ground, for the same price we had paid for a tiny one-bedroom flat in Brighton. We were spending most of our weekends at that time driving our beloved vintage Rover 100 through the Derbyshire Dales.

We loved Buxton, with its domed buildings, tea-rooms, hotels, pavilion gardens and best of all, the splendid Frank Matcham Theatre - it was like a mini Scala Milan. We found here however that we had to serve an apprenticeship to be accepted into the community - very unlike Hurstpierpoint.

We now had two Airedales, which behaved impeccably in the flat. Not so impeccably, however, that I felt able to ask the other residents if they would mind me putting a couple of donkeys in the garage.

Keith was getting on fine with the donkeys, although he was growing a little weary with having to serve them breakfast at four in the morning, which was the only way to silence their braying. He was also grateful for the supply of free manure, which was doing wonders for his vegetable patch - "you could grow roses on lino with this stuff", as he put it - but he was now beginning to run out of places to spread it.

I drove to nearby Bakewell and had a chat with John Scott, senior planning officer at the National Peak Park. I told him I was thinking of moving the location for my new film from Devon to the Peak District. At the same time I had to find somewhere to house my two donkeys.

John had a suggestion. For the past 16 years there had been an enforcement order on a dilapidated house called Pictor Hall, just outside Buxton. We drove out to take a look.

The place turned out to be quite spectacular. It could have come straight from the pages of a novel by one of the Brontë sisters.

Behind the house was a run-down quadrangle, with stables where the gentry had obviously once kept the horses and carriages. It had a hay barn and 20 stable boxes. As the estate agents say, it was full of potential. It seemed the place belonged to an elderly lady called Miss Fearn, whose father had left it to her.

I decided to ask Miss Fearn through her solicitor if I could rent the stables for six months. It turned out that the solicitor was Martin Brooke-Taylor, elder brother of the comedian Tim Brooke-Taylor, the comedian - a comforting show business link.

Martin was in favour of the plan and agreed to put it to Miss Fearn. After much further discussion and exchange of paperwork, we finally got our stables. Keith and Maria and their children had by now become very attached to our donkeys - in fact, we named him Danny after their son - so it was with mixed feelings that they waved them off a few weeks later.

The donkeys took a little while to adjust to their new surroundings, though we did our best to encourage them with plenty of feed and hay. After that, we let them settle in with the minimum fuss.

Now that we had removed the lice and maggots and given them both medicated baths, the donkeys were getting their lovely coats back. We realised that Baz had the most beautiful champagne ears. The scars around his shoulders and under his belly from the leather harness he had been forced to wear were healing well.

Danny, on the other hand, preferred to live as Baz's shadow. He would follow him everywhere, mimicking his every move. We noticed that he was always shaking his head and banging into things and would spend long periods just walking round and round in circles. So we made our first call to the vet.

It seemed that Danny had been beaten badly around the head for sustained periods. He had lost the sight of one eye, and the constant smacking had made him suffer headaches, which was why he liked to keep rotating. His nerves were bad, and he would need a lot of care in the next few months.

Baz had endured much the same experience - and more worryingly, he had developed septicaemia under his belly, where there were still pieces of harness dug in under the skin.

It came as a shock to realise just what people were capable of doing to these poor, defenceless animals. And we couldn't help thinking that Baz and Danny could hardly be the only ones - there must be many more donkeys out there who had suffered similar cruelty at the hands of heartless owners and animal traders. But there was absolutely nothing we could do about it. At least, not yet.

I now had the daunting task of raising some finance to enable us to keep our two donkeys in the manner to which they had become accustomed. It was time to go back to work.

Chapter 16

Donizetti and Dot Cotton

The obvious place to look for some fresh theatre work was right on our doorstep in Buxton, which was home to an excellent theatrical tradition. I went to see Malcolm Fraser, the artistic director. I put to him a proposition which I thought might save him having to go to London to hunt for ideas.

I asked him to give me a fortnight to come up with two special concerts for that year's Festival. He was impressed by my portfolio and luckily for me had heard of my work, so he agreed. I went to work, keeping music as my main theme but inserting some unusual angles.

My first idea was to present a show called *A Masterclass on Donizetti,* the Italian composer who would dominate that year's festival, notably with a production of *Lucia di Lammermoor.* I would use the Camarata orchestra of 40 musicians and gather three of the finest opera singers I could lure away from the Royal Opera House Convent Garden. They were Louise Winter, Anthony Michaels-Moore and Amanda Roocroft, an up-and-coming young soprano. I kept it to three singers as I wanted to reserve my main budget for the host of the night – June Brown.

June was best known for her *EastEnders* character Dot Cotton, the nosey busybody from the launderette who was fast becoming a British institution with her bible in her overalls and her chain smoking. I spent some time on the phone to June's agent, who very much wanted her to take part but had enormous difficulty getting her released from *EastEnders.* Finally, at

Chapter 16

June's own insistence, she was granted one week off.

I went back to the Buxton Festival office and told Malcolm about my plan.

He went pale.

"Are you absolutely certain this will work?" he stammered.

"Absolutely" I said. I had no doubts whatsoever that it would indeed work.

I knew June to be one of this country's most cherished character actresses with a wonderful voice and a tremendous talent and ability. Her Cleopatra had been world renowned, long before *EastEnders* was conceived. But like Malcolm, the audience didn't know about all that, and this, I told him, was my big surprise.

My enthusiasm made Malcolm relax a little, though I'm sure he still thought I was unhinged.

"What's the next step?" he asked.

"I'll go and introduce myself to June and talk to her about it all" I said. Malcolm was horrified that I didn't even know her. I'm sure he was secretly hoping that she would say no.

June was an actress who liked a challenge - she enjoyed taking risks. She had been in *EastEnders* now for many years and loved to be offered contrasting work to test her ability and activate her brain.

Believe me, there is nothing wrong with June's brain. She finishes the *Telegraph* crossword most mornings in 15 minutes. And don't even consider playing Trivial Pursuit with her - she wins every time. However, that did not mean her knowledge of opera would be up to tackling such a project without a certain amount of work.

"Yes dear, I love the idea of doing a Masterclass, it sounds like great fun.

Chapter 16

But I don't know very much about Donny Osmond."

"Donizetti" I corrected.

"Even less, dear" she said.

I told her something about Donizetti. She told me I would have to write the Masterclass and send her a cassette to learn. I agreed.

"OK then. I'll look forward to it" she said.

I kissed her on both cheeks and told her how thrilled I was.

I went back to Buxton and got the committee's approval to write and produce the Masterclass. It took me seven weeks. The research and the script were over 300 pages long.

The Committee were now feeling rather happier, as the concert had sold out immediately. As I'd hoped, the title alone had sold the seats.

June was not so happy when she saw the reams of script she would have to learn. She suggested that the only way to do it was to write it on a set of postcards.

You wouldn't think it possible, but we pulled it off. The concert was a huge success. June Brown became our close friend, and the Masterclass brought me a cheque for £5000 to start building a new home for my donkeys.

When June learned why I had put on her Masterclass, she asked if she could come and meet my donkeys. Annie and I drove her up to Pictor Hall and took her to the stables. She marvelled at what we were doing. June spent an hour with the donkeys, saying how relaxed they were making her feel.

My next show was aimed at young musicians and was to be called *Overture and Beginners*. For this I needed to build a full orchestra of 73 youngsters,

Chapter 16

all Grade 8 and all under the age of sixteen.

I travelled to Paris to ask the multiple-Oscar-winning composer Michel Legrand if he would consider coming to England for my show. Michel was interested, but he explained that it would difficult - he was booked for years ahead. However he did have one weekend free - and it just happened that it was the last weekend of the Buxton Festival. I couldn't believe my luck.

I arranged for an English conductor and friend of his, Cyril Ornadel, to help by working with the youngsters for the preceding week. Cyril was concerned that these children, proficient as they were at their own level, would not be able to cope with the scores. But these kids were talented. The auditions had been fiercely contested. The major schools like Cheetham and the Royal Northern College had put forward all their best students.

Cyril placed his young orchestra in a huge semi-circle and took a deep breath. "Good morning, ladies and gentlemen" he said.

"Good morning sir" they responded, in perfect unison.

"Have you any idea what you're up against here?" he asked.

"No sir" came 73 honest answers.

He proceeded to tell them just how accomplished a figure Michel Legrand was - and what a challenge it would be to play under his direction. Then he showed them clips from some of Michel's films, such as *The Thomas Crown Affair*. They sat silently through them, looking rather dazed. Cyril now showed them how to negotiate the score - all 21 pages of it.

Needless to say, the next few minutes were pretty chaotic. There were screeches and scratches, bum notes, dropped scores, tempos lost without trace. At the end, Cyril put his baton down and surveyed the anguished youngsters. At this point I feared I was going to be hanged, drawn and quartered for suggesting the whole idea in the first place.

"I expected that sort of performance first time" he said. "But you did actually manage to play it more or less as written. I am confident that you will be able to pull this off. Many, many congratulations!"

I tried to build a big show round Michel. I brought his compatriot Sacha Distel in from Paris and Jack Jones from the States. I brought the Swingle Singers over - one of the group was Michel's sister - and I got our own Vince Hill to sing some of Michel's stage numbers. Jane Lapotaire, who had just starred as Edith Piaf, agreed to host the night.

Michel Legrand had written *Ne me quittez pas* for Piaf (he had been her accompanist), so we arranged for Jane to sing it on the night. She was terrified of what he might think of her performance.

When Michel flew in from Paris in his private jet he insisted on going straight to meet his orchestra and demanding a full run through. He was thrilled by this marvellous young symphony orchestra. At the end of the first session, he was so moved that tears ran down his face. He had never expected them to be so good.

"Now my children, tomorrow we are going to break it all down into sections" he said. "We can then work on all the little intricacies that are missing at present. Listen to what I am going to say to you all very carefully. You are all magnificent, but you are young. I now have to make you feel what you are playing. My job now is to make you interpret my work, my scores, my music with passion and sex." Laughter ran around the hall. But over the next day and a half, Michel made the youngsters work until their fingers bled.

The Buxton audience and all the local dignitaries were spellbound by the show. When Michel walked down the centre aisle through the stalls and climbed on to the stage to his podium, the audience raised the roof. There must have been a good five minutes of welcoming applause, which made him feel very much at home. He made his orchestra stand to show how proud he was of them.

The women in the audience went crazy when Sacha Distel made his entrance down the centre aisle. Jack Jones told a good joke about his father's number one hit *Donkey Serenade* which I particularly appreciated. Vince Hill, the Swingle Singers and Jane Lapotaire were all wonderful. But my greatest pleasure was at the end of the concert when Michel introduced each and every one of our young musicians by name.

Michel was so impressed by our young drummer that he invited him back to Paris to play in his jazz club. Many others went on to do work in symphony orchestras around the world.

Funnily enough, that was it for me and Buxton. The festival organisers had very little to say to me after the show, and they never asked me to do anything for the event again. Frankly, I don't think they liked me having such a success with *Overture and Beginners* - perhaps they felt it had stolen the thunder from the operas. But so many lovely letters and cards came in from the public that I had no doubt what a success it had been for both the festival and the town.

My donkeys certainly enjoyed the concert, or rather the benefits of the money it raised for them. Such was the publicity that they became overnight celebrities. Afterwards Jane Lapotaire asked if she could come up and meet my four-legged friends.

Among those whose attention was drawn to my work at Pictor Hall were the RSPCA, who told me there were lots of other donkeys needing comfortable homes, and wondered if I could take some of them in. We agreed to take four donkeys, so now we had three stables full.

Children were also beginning to visit, many of them with special needs. All in all the stables were getting rather busy, and with Annie's costume work and my writing we were both now getting very tired.

The animal welfare organisations had now discovered us, and within six months our donkey family had risen to eighteen. There were 'orphans', donkeys belonging to elderly folk who had been rendered homeless on the demise of their owners. There were divorce cases, when the husband and wife refused to share the donkey so that it had to be found an independent home. And of course, there were always more donkeys being rescued from a squalid fate in the meat trade.

We were astonished to learn how much donkeys love each other. There were very few altercations between them. The only time there was any sense of competition was when the feed buckets came out. They would graze peacefully, always in their own groups. The elders always took a great interest in the upbringing of the younger members.

There was however a definite pecking order, and I was heartened to see Baz win his stripes by becoming the unchallenged boss. He led the growing herd with great dignity and sensibility. He would convene donkey committee meetings, at which all the important decisions seemed to be made under his chairmanship.

Baz was also extremely patient and caring with Danny, who was by now not at all right in the head. He became a great worry to us all. He would kick and bite us, or charge at us for no apparent reason.

Every afternoon people would visit the donkeys. Bags of carrots were dropped off daily, along with boxes of polo mints, extra strong mints and their favourites, Fisherman's Friends.

A teacher at the John Duncan School for special needs children in Buxton rang to ask if they could bring their children up to spend some time with us at the stables. We agreed - and learned an important lesson. These animals had a natural affinity for children. Their patience and calmness made them safe and reassuring to be with. The therapeutic value of bringing donkeys and children together became more and more evident.

Unfortunately, the stable area was not really suitable for youngsters to be wandering around, and it wasn't long before the health and safety people stepped in. They were not prepared to allow children with disabilities to visit the premises as they stood. The ground was muddy and uneven. There were no walkways. The stables were old and not as yet finished to the required standard. We still had a lot of work to do.

So with great sadness, we closed off the stables to visitors. Some very special children found it hard to forgive us for that.

We didn't know it yet, but in fact a solution was just around the corner.

Chapter 17

Anneka to the rescue

One day that September, the phone rang. "Mr Stirling, my name is Tom" said the caller. "I run a company called Menthor Films. I produce a programme called *Challenge Anneka*.

"We've received a letter from a special needs teacher in Buxton, challenging us to help you with your derelict stables. It would be an ideal subject matter for one of our programmes. With your permission, I'd like to talk about how we could be of best use to you. What do you think?"

I was rather taken aback, but I thanked him and said that I would naturally be more than willing to accept this kind offer.

He explained that in setting up the programme it was imperative that Anneka herself should know nothing about the challenge beforehand. The crew had to record the surprise as it happened. If it leaked out in any way they would have to abandon the project.

When Tom came up to meet us, he was completely smitten with the place. He thought it might well turn out to be one of the series' biggest challenges, but felt the rewards should be well worth the effort and expense.

Anneka and her crew would set out to transform the whole stable area. They would rebuild and make safe all 26 of the stables. They would lay on an electricity supply and a water supply, build walkways and rebuild the hay barn with a new roof. The only thing they wouldn't do was build toilets. Not good television!

Miss Fearn agreed to the plan. She could see that what they were offering was the perfect way to get her property off the enforcement list. Tom even offered to rebuild her farm entrance and the little bridge by the A6, as it was not safe for their vehicles to cross. They would make good her tracks and resurface her cow barn. No wonder she was happy.

When Anneka arrived at the Palace Hotel in Buxton with her camera crew, all she had to go on was my phone number on her desk. I was told to respond to her call by inviting her to the stables, without giving her any information about the Challenge.

Anneka duly found her way to Pictor Hall and Annie and I led her through the grounds to the stables, where she was met by eighteen surprised donkeys.

"Oh my god - donkeys! I love donkeys!" she said directly to camera. That was enough for Tom. The look of surprise on her face was just what he needed.

"What are they all doing here?" she asked.

I explained the whole story, trying to ignore the TV camera pointing up my nose and the sound operator crouched at my feet. I told her about the animal rescues, the children and the therapeutic value of the donkeys. She took it all in.

"And my challenge is?"

"To build us a stable where children with special needs and donkeys can get to know each other and gain from one another."

"How absolutely lovely!" she said.

Chapter 17

Now that the cat was out of the bag, the whole production crew appeared around her as if from nowhere. They went into action without delay. Up rolled the *Challenge Anneka* lorry, which until now had been covered in trees and bushes to camouflage it. Up came the outside broadcast vehicles with lighting and sound. Anneka's mobile production office was parked in the middle of the stable area. The speed of the setup was amazing.

The work and the filming had to be completed in three days and two nights. They lit the whole compound so that the day crew could be followed by a night shift, with no delay in between. There were hundreds of people to muster and tons of materials to collect, most of it donated by generous local businesses which enjoyed the publicity.

Anneka was extremely professional and very capable. She had the backup of a huge publicity machine which was put in place to attract contributions in return for publicity without advertising too blatantly. She could work out who was going to play ball and who wasn't in seconds.

On the first day the crew were up before dawn. The first of 27 concrete mixing lorries were already waiting in convoy to deliver quick-drying concrete. A gang of labourers, builders and brickies who had been on the job since 4 am were tucking into a giant cooked breakfast. A dozen carpenters had already taken off the stable doors, and the electricians were busy installing wiring to the boxes.

Dumper trucks were gathering up the wood and flattening the ground so that the concrete could be laid. The roofers were starting on the haybarn roof and a team of six dry-stone wallers were building a full-length perimeter wall.

I was staggered to see how much Anneka had managed to do in a single afternoon. She had already been on the road for the last hour and a half collecting donations of brooms, rakes, shovels, buckets and tea towels from the neighbouring towns.

Chapter 17

A man came all the way from Kent with a beautiful donkey cart he had made for us. Someone from a hatter's in Oxford brought 50 children's riding hats. A lady from Somerset had made 100 rosettes for the occasion. A local artist who specialised in canal boats came to create paintings over each of the stable doors. Local farmers donated hay and straw.

Miss Fearn seemed to be enjoying every minute of it. She took full advantage of the catering by joining us for each of the three daily meals served in the marquees.

By the time they had all finished, we had the finest stables this side of Newmarket. The 67 builders, drivers, carpenters, wallers, brickies, painters, plumbers and electricians stood in the quadrangle while Anneka climbed on to a JCB to tell them what an extraordinary achievement it was. She had put her own heart and soul into the venture and was clearly very tired - she wasn't the only one.

Anneka had insisted that the John Duncan School, which had initiated the whole thing, should be invited to open the stables. If the teacher there had not made that phone call, none of this would have happened. We welcomed a coachload of children to the ceremony and each child was given an adoption certificate for one of the donkeys.

A huge carrot cake was wheeled in to celebrate the opening. Each builder and workman was able to lead a donkey with a child around the ring, which proved very moving.

After everyone had left that evening, Anneka and the camera crew stayed on to film some atmospheric shots of the donkeys exploring their newly-refurbished five-star homes. Anneka went home happy, and our programme became one of the two most watched in the entire series.

And then - disaster. A few weeks after it was broadcast, Miss Fearn, having had most of her farm rebuilt for nothing, her bridge mended and her barn entrances reconcreted, announced that she was throwing us out. She wanted her stables back.

We couldn't believe it. The benefits she had gained from our work were incalculable.

She gave Annie, me and the donkeys - we now had 59 of them - four weeks to vacate the premises, as of course she was legally entitled to do. She didn't seem to mind how unpopular this made her with us. It was an appalling slap in the face for all of those who had laboured so hard to bring the project off.

I went back to Pictor Hall one evening some ten years later and looked over the walls to see how the stables were looking. I was horrified to see that the whole place was once again dirty and derelict, with nothing but a few cows grazing forlornly in the weeds. The work we had done had simply been abandoned to nature. I felt upset all over again for Anneka and her team, thinking how hard they had worked.

So now we were penniless, and 59 donkeys were homeless. No other offers of accommodation were forthcoming. We felt alone, miserable and angry. But somehow, we had to find a way forward.

Chapter 18

Birth of a Trust

We looked everywhere for a new home for our donkeys. I drove around Derbyshire, surveying empty farms and derelict barns from Hathersage to the Goyt Valley, but I could find nothing we could possibly afford which would serve our purpose.

Then one day, I decided on an impulse to break off my homeward drive in the hamlet of Wormhill, a couple of miles from Pictor Hall, for a pot of tea. Yvonne, the owner of the tea shop, recognised me and said how sorry she was over what had happened to my stables. We got chatting, and she said she knew of an abandoned barn and shippon (an old word for a cow shed) just a couple of hundred yards down the lane. Would I like to take a look?

I didn't need to be asked twice. I plodded along the lane and sure enough, there at the end of it was a large barn and a shippon, entirely deserted. I'd been searching the four corners of the county for a new home for my donkeys, and it looked as if I'd found one right on my doorstep.

Yvonne made an appointment for me that evening to meet the owner, Tim Bagshaw at Wormhill Hall. Tim and I got on splendidly. We would have to respect the buildings as they were listed and any work would need consent, even if we could afford it. We would also have to respect the privacy of Tim's parents, who lived close to the barn - along with their geese, which, he warned me, were doing a good job as watchdogs.

Chapter 18

Apart from that it was all fairly straightforward. We were able to move the donkeys to their new home on foot, which required one volunteer for every donkey. That was quite a spectacle, particularly when 400 people turned out to watch. They even rang the church bells for us.

We had to be very wary of the geese, which would attack anything and anyone in their path. They soon quietened down, though; I have a feeling Baz had a word with them. It's extraordinary the way animals communicate with one another.

By the time I had I rented an additional ten-acre meadow from Tim for grazing, we were up to 67 donkeys. They were not popular with everyone. I was dismayed by the attitude of some of the local motorists, who would use the lane as a short cut and could not bear to be kept waiting by a line of gently-plodding donkeys on their way to graze. Some of the drivers would try to push them on with their bumpers. Annie got bruised several times by passing wing mirrors, and one young man even drove straight at her. Most, fortunately, were patient and courteous.

Neither Annie nor I were now working and we were down to our last few shillings. It was clear that if we were going to be able to carry on running Wormhill, we would have to open it to the paying public.

It was at this point that we came up with the idea of setting up a registered charity for our donkey sanctuary, and forming a trust to run it. It didn't take long to realise that there was only one possible name for it - the Michael Elliott Trust.

Michael Elliott was the man who had directed me in my first television play, and he had been a huge influence on my career, as on those of many. He had also been a very important figure to Annie, who had spent ten years working for him at the Royal Exchange Theatre in Manchester. Michael had died in 1984 at the age of 53, just as he had been about to take over the directorship of the National Theatre from Sir Laurence

Olivier, who had chosen him as his successor. His passing had been a great shock, and a huge loss, to the acting profession.

Now, seven years later, we had an opportunity to create something in his memory. Michael had loved working with both children and animals, so I felt sure he would have appreciated our plan.

Setting up the trust required the processing of a mountain of paperwork, and more importantly finding trustees, directors and patrons. Vanessa Redgrave and Alan Bates, both of whom had cottages in the Peaks, were very supportive of the idea - and very generous in supporting it.

I called a meeting at the Palace Hotel in Buxton to try to put the whole project in motion. June Brown travelled up from London along with Jane Lapotaire, Brian Cox and many of Michael's old friends and colleagues.

I could not believe the response from the world of theatre. Within a month we had a list of patrons that was longer than the cast list for the average West End show. Twenty-two of the best-known names in the entertainment world had committed themselves to our humble cause - Anthony Andrews, Richard Attenborough, Ian Bannen, Brian Blessed, Tony Britton, June Brown, Marti Caine, Bobby Charlton, Roald Dahl, Judi Dench, Michael Denison, Marianne Elliott (Michael's daughter), Edward Fox, Dulcie Gray, Alec Guinness, Patricia Hayes, Jane Lapotaire, John Mills, Stefanie Powers, David Puttnam, Paul Scofield and Michael Williams. Quite extraordinary.

Jane Lapotaire agreed to be our president for the first year, and she did a marvellous job. She then handed over to June Brown, who accepted the post permanently - she is still doing it, bless her.

The whole team have now put in over 20 years, except of course for those we have lost - Alec Guinness, John Mills, Marti Caine, Michael Williams,

Roald Dahl, Michael Denison and Ian Bannen. They will all be long remembered for much more than their work in entertainment.

After John Mills died in 2005 we were delighted to welcome his daughter Hayley in his place. Along the years since we have been lucky enough to be joined by Martin Shaw, Jenny Seagrove, Chris de Burgh, Pam Ayres and Bill Kenwright.

Our first priority in creating the Michael Elliott Trust was to raise the funds we so urgently needed to pay for looking after all those donkeys. That meant publicity. I reasoned that the best way of achieving that was to trade on my show business experiences to develop an interesting talk which I could deliver to women's institutes, mother's unions, Probus clubs and the like.

I prepared it by stringing together a series of anecdotes from my life in the theatre, culminating in the story of how we had got involved with donkeys. I decided to save the harsh realities of the plight of donkeys until the end - after all, I needed to give people as much reason as possible to dig into their pockets to help us once I'd finished talking.

The talks went down well and began to bring in much-needed funds. We sold donkey scarves, donkey pens and donkey T-shirts. Pam Ayres wrote a lovely poem about a donkey coming to the Trust, which I had printed on tea towels.

One element that was missing from my presentation was a real live donkey. I decided to put that right, and recruited a badly-abused animal called Pepsi, who was pure brown with a stunning black cross over his shoulders, a gentle face and delightful hazel eyes. I had matched him with a piebald donkey called Oxo, a very attractive piebald (brown and white) jenny, and things were going well between them.

Chapter 18

I took Pepsi to churches, cathedrals, garden parties, fetes, schools - anywhere where there was a gathering, to get him used to large crowds. As he got used to people I started taking him to noisier places, and invested in a Land Rover and trailer to make the travelling easier. He would stand beside me at the presentations resplendent in his coat, specially made for him by Annie with his name on, and his custom-made bridle and rosette. He certainly looked the part. But his beloved Oxo didn't appreciate his absences and he was always very happy to get back to her.

We managed to get into some extraordinary places. There was the time a woman asked us to take Pepsi to see her husband, who was in a cancer ward in Stockport Hospital. She couldn't see any problem about taking a donkey up three floors in a lift and walking it to the ward. So I said we would give it a go.

However, it wasn't as simple as that. The matron insisted that Pepsi should wrapped in Cellophane from muzzle to tail to avoid any problems with contamination.

I think that must be the only time in history when a donkey has been marched through a hospital swaddled in Cellophane, closely followed by a porter with a dustpan and brush just in case of an accident. Pepsi was of course as good as gold, and there were no accidents – then or at any other time in his touring career.

Pepsi did a charity walk from Sheffield to Buxton with Annie, to commemorate Marti Caine's work at the Trust. He walked coast-to-coast from Scarborough to Blackpool with a party of children - 327 miles in three weeks (more on that in Chapter 20.) He appeared at the Opera House in Buxton for Cancer Research. He appeared on June Brown's Christmas video of *Little Donkey*, which Terry Wogan tipped as his number one – it didn't achieve the top spot but it did do the Trust a great deal of good.

Chapter 18

In the ten years Pepsi was my partner on the road, he never so much as scratched a parquet floor. He trusted me implicitly, and I in turn loved him to bits.

Don't ever imagine donkeys aren't intelligent. Pepsi could tell when the end of my talk was approaching by my presentation photographs - when he saw that I'd reached a particular blue image towards the end, he would start to get himself ready to meet the audience.

Many's the time someone would ask him to sign a copy of my book about the trust. In the end I got a printer friend to make me an ink 'hoof print' for the purpose.

Another original idea for raising money came through our friendship with Bill Eley, a highly accomplished local artist. When Bill painted a stunning portrait of a donkey called Herbie we had 2000 Christmas cards printed with it on the front. They sold out in eight weeks. Bill would also sketch newly-arrived donkeys warts-and-all to show just dreadful their treatment had been, and follow it up with further paintings as their condition improved. This enabled us to prepare collages showing how each animal had recovered all the way from a badly-beaten wreck to a fit and healthy animal. We still have those images, as a vivid illustration of the work we do.

When Bill married a former model of his called Jenny, Annie was only too pleased to make an outfit for her. But the real star of the occasion was Herbie, who attended the ceremony in a fetching coat and collar which Annie had run up for him.

When Herbie died a few months later – he was an old donkey, nearly 40 – the news came as a terrible shock to poor Bill. It was a year before he could bring himself to come back to the Trust. He still keeps in touch, but as he says, there will only ever be one Herbie.

Chapter 18

It's always a great privilege to welcome special needs children to the Trust. They make the sanctuary come alive with happiness. It is quite extraordinary to see how sensitive the donkeys are to these children. If a child falls, the whole line of donkeys stops. If a child is struggling, the donkey takes it slowly. In the company of children they rarely pull their heads down to graze, and they never bolt.

The efforts the children make are another eye opener. They may be confined to wheelchairs or on callipers, and sometimes they have serious vision or hearing problems. They could be suffering autism, spina bifida or Downs syndrome, yet however serious the disability we hear never a complaint or a harsh word.

Among the people I met through our work was Judy Dunlop, a teacher at a special needs school in Chesterfield. One day she brought along her son Blair, a very bright and talented 11-year-old whom I liked enormously. Blair loved the donkeys and became particularly attached to our founder and leader, Baz.

He also proved to be have a marvellous understanding of the children who came to the Trust and was particularly skilled at dealing with a 14-year-old who suffered from a very rare condition called Cri du Chat syndrome. This boy suffered from an excess of nervous energy and would rush wildly about, heedless of all attempts to calm him.

I will never forget the time I watched Blair introduce this boy to a donkey called Joshua. An astonishing change took place. Blair showed him how to stroke the donkey's mane and muzzle and the boy who had never previously been known to sit still for more than two seconds sat calmly watching the donkey for a full 15 minutes.

Judy was a folk singer when she wasn't teaching, and Blair's father Ashley Hutchings was a towering figure in the music world, having founded

Chapter 18

several of the UK's biggest folk bands. It seemed that Blair had inherited the urge to be a performer. He was intrigued by my background, and one day he approached me to ask my advice about a career in entertainment.

Judy told me there was a private school in Derby which specialised in drama and would be ideal for Blair – but somehow he would have to get a scholarship, as they couldn't afford the fees.

I offered to help. As chairman of the Michael Elliott Trust, I wrote to the school explaining how strongly we felt Blair deserved a chance to go there. June Brown, who was very impressed by Blair, added her own note. It did the trick, and we got Blair his place.

That year I produced our annual Michael Elliott Trust Awards at The SAS Radisson Hotel at Manchester Airport. These awards are an opportunity for the profession to honour their own. Among the award recipients that evening were Martin Shaw, Sandy Toksvig, Ainsley Harriott, Sally Whittaker, John Bardon, Michelle Collins, Sarah Parish, Jesse Wallace, Bill Kenwright and Jenny Seagrove.

The proceeds of the night were going to the charity, so I needed a way of presenting the work of the Trust to an audience of 400 distinguished theatrical guests. I decided to make a video of the donkeys at work with the children. As Blair appeared in some of the footage, I asked him to say a few words to welcome the guests and acquaint them with the work of the Trust. I offered to provide him with a script, but he said he would prefer to write it himself.

Blair spoke for ten minutes, all in his own words. At the end everybody was in floods of tears, including Annie and me. He explained what the Trust meant to him and what it had achieved, and finished with some harrowing accounts of rescues. I was so glad I had put my nervousness to one side and let him write it himself. The audience rose to him and gave him a standing ovation.

Chapter 18

Blair's first step into the entertainment world was an audition for the movie *Charlie and the Chocolate Factory* with Johnny Depp. From hundreds of applicants for the role of Charlie, it was finally down to a choice between him and Freddie Highmore. In the end Freddie was chosen, but Blair did get the part of Willie Wonka as a boy.

I introduced Blair to the London agent Derek Webster, and his career began to take off. Today, barely 18, he has already become an accomplished singer and guitarist.

Chapter 19

A roof over our heads

Wormhill made a wonderful new home for our donkeys, but we had reckoned without the success that our growing fame would bring. The better known the sanctuary became, the more donkeys we were asked to take on. Visitors came flooding in, blocking lanes and churning up grass verges with their cars. Barely eighteen months after the move, we found ourselves faced with an unpalatable truth – we were going to need somewhere bigger.

Fortunately, this time I didn't have to scour the county for a solution. I had already noticed that a place called Lodesbarn Farm, in the village of Peak Forest a couple of miles away from Wormhill, had come on to the market. The barns were in a poor state, but the place had 30 acres of land, which more than made up for that. There would be enough space for Annie and me to live there alongside the donkeys, which had never been possible with our other sanctuaries. It was well off the beaten track, secluded and safe for the children, and the nearest neighbour was two miles away, so our charges would be able to bray to their hearts' content without bothering anybody.

I felt great sympathy for the owners – it hadn't been their choice to put the place on the market, but their farming business had collapsed. They seemed keen on our enterprise, which they thought would help to ensure Lodesbarn's future.

Chapter 19

The survey revealed that the mineral rights were still in the hands of the Duke of Devonshire. It occurred to me that to win the interest and support of the Duchess – who is deeply respected in the county - would do no harm whatsoever, so I contacted Chatsworth House.

To my delight, the Duchess took a great interest in our project and we went to see the place together. She agreed that it would be perfect for us, and said so to the owners, which I hope helped them to feel a little better about having to give it up.

Now we faced the small matter of raising the £200,000 we would need to buy it. We had been through a difficult patch and had no funds of our own. June Brown drove up from London and we sat down to try to work out a plan of action to purchase Lodesbarn.

We wrote to our patrons and to various trusts and givers of grants. Finally we were able, through our charity, to put down a deposit and raise a mortgage.

Lodesbarn Farm was a tremendous find, but it was extraordinarily remote for a couple who were used to the bright lights and a busy social round. It took Annie and me quite a while to adjust. It wasn't so bad in the daytime, when we could appreciate the space and the spectacular views, but when night fell we felt dreadfully isolated. It seemed as if we had marooned ourselves on our own private desert island, miles from civilisation and friendly faces.

The donkeys didn't see it that way. They had never been happier or safer. Nor did our young visitors, whom we could look after in peace and privacy.

At first Annie and I had to manage living in one room, such was the state of the rest of the place. We were tremendously lucky to have our little band of volunteer builders, electricians and plumbers, all willing to give up their precious weekends to help get the place into shape.

The Prince's Trust stepped in early on with a wonderful conservation scheme sponsored by Sainsbury's. Thirteen youngsters, along with a similar number of disabled young people, set to work protecting the land around the farm with fencing and walls. Not only did they put up something like a mile of fencing, they raised the funds to buy the materials, the fence posts, the gates, and everything else that was needed. They turned our little wood into a nature reserve.

They were all enchanting youngsters with a zest for life and a strong community spirit. In the evenings they would light campfires and play their guitars. Many were from poor backgrounds, some were disabled and others had learning difficulties, but they all worked together to see the project though. Some months later we were privileged to meet Prince Charles and to tell him how thrilled we were with what the Trust had achieved for us.

It wasn't easy to persuade the world that our problems were behind us after three moves in a few years. But we had a lot of money to raise, so we had to win all the fans and supporters we could. There was the farmhouse to be gutted and refurbished, the barn to be rebuilt and 50 stables to create. We also had to get on top of the land and tackle urgent jobs like ragwort clearance.

So I put my producer's cap firmly back on. I started by calling the opera singer Lesley Garrett and asking her to do a concert for us at the City Hall in Sheffield. Lesley was born and bred in Doncaster and is fiercely proud of her northern roots. She was also a friend of Marti Caine's and had been very impressed by Marti's hard work for our trust.

I asked Lesley if there was any musical aim she was still looking to fulfil - a tall order, as she had already sung in all the greatest halls with the world's top musicians. But it seemed there was one ambition she had never realised. What she really wanted to do was sing with the Black Dyke Mills Brass Band.

I contacted the band's musical director and went along to see them in rehearsal. I was blown away by their passion and virtuosity. But would they be able to tackle the classical operatic material Lesley would be singing?

"Piece of cake" came the reply. "This band can play anything." And he was right, of course. In the event the band played the first half of the concert, then Lesley joined them for the second half.

My experience has taught me that if you give a well-known and talented artist a chance to tackle something different, the stimulus of an adventure into unknown territory usually delivers a great performance. That concert was no exception. Lesley and her new friends in the Black Dyke Mills Band performed that night to a packed house.

She and some of the musicians visited us the next day to see for themselves the work we were doing. Not only were we able to pay off a large slice of the mortgage we'd had to raise for the sanctuary, but we could start the restoration work on the barn and put a new roof and chimneys on the farmhouse.

My next project for the sanctuary was another concert, this time based on Enid Blyton's Famous Five. *Local Heroes* would be the title. It occurred to me to ask David Puttnam if he would contact the musician Mark Knopfler, who had written the sound track of the film David had produced of the same name. I knew Marti had been a huge fan of Mark's. David kindly agreed to write to him.

One Saturday morning at the Trust, the phone rang. One of my most valued volunteers was on duty that day. I shall call her Mavis.

Chapter 19

"It's Mark Knopfler here" said the caller. "May I speak to John Stirling?"

"I'm sorry, he's busy mucking out the donkeys" said Mavis. "Can I take a message?"

"Just tell him Mark Knopfler called, would you?" said the world-famous musician.

"Can you spell that for me?" she asked.

The four-times Grammy winner spelled his name for her, and she wrote it down.

"Mr Stirling's very busy you know" said Mavis to the man who has sold 120 million albums and holds three honorary doctorates in music. "If you're ringing to sponsor a donkey or book a birthday party for your kids, I'm sure I can deal with it."

"OK" said Mark. "I just wanted Mr Stirling to know that I'm happy to do a concert for his trust, if he'd like to book somewhere. But please tell him I have only one free date, seven weeks on Sunday."

"Ooh, I can do that for you" said Mavis. "It's me that deals with all the Women's Institutes and Mother's Unions. I can get you a hall, no problem. Just leave it with me for a few hours."

Mavis then decided, very considerately, not to trouble me with all this information but to take care of the stranger's request herself. She booked a local hall, organised stalls with second-hand books, a tombola and a raffle and arranged tea and scones. Then she rang Mark back to tell him about the arrangements.

"I've booked the village hall at Ashford in the Water for you and your friends to play" she told the guitarist who had played with Bob Dylan, Eric Clapton, Elton John, Kris Kristofferson and Emmy Lou Harris. "I'm sure you'll love it. It seats 60, but you can get 70 in if you're pushed."

"I'm sure it's a very nice hall" said the singer who had once headlined a concert at Wembley Stadium which had been broadcast to 600 million people. "But I think I should warn you, we do have rather a lot of equipment. Three truckloads, actually."

There was a pause while Mavis tried to take this in. "So what sort of place do you think you'd need for this... musical evening of yours?" she asked him.

"How about the Arena in Sheffield?" he suggested. "19,000 seats. That should be enough. Or we might just squeeze into the City Hall."

Having put the phone down, Mavis then decided that the time might have come to mention her negotiations with the strange Mr Knopfler to me.

"WHAT!" I screamed. "Don't you know who he is - Dire Straits! They're the biggest rock band in the world!"

"We'll all be in dire straits if we do what he's suggesting" countered Mavis.

I got on the phone to Mark as fast as I could, and did some serious grovelling. Mark, of course, was fine about the whole thing. He said he would like to do the show with his country band, the Notting Hillbillies.

Mark and his Hillbillies did a wonderful concert at the City Hall and we packed them to the rafters. The Searchers opened the show for us by treating us to their 1960s and 70s hits.

I had asked one of our patrons, Ian Bannen, to introduce Mark and his band. Ian was received with a great cheer from the crowd as he walked on. He looked in complete control, but within a few seconds disaster threatened - I could see that he had forgotten Mark's name. Fortunately he had several thousand Dire Straits fans in front of him to shout the prompt.

Chapter 19

Mark dedicated a number from *Local Hero, Annie's Song*, to my Annie, which pleased her immensely as she adores the song.

The concert made a lot of money. Mark auctioned the guitar he'd been playing, complete with signature, and gave us a second one to raffle. The two instruments raised over £8000 between them - enough to pay for the construction of 23 stables.

With two profitable concerts in a year, we seemed to be heading in the right direction. The improvements we were making were bringing back the supporters. Unfortunately 1998 continued on a much sadder note, with a series of tragic losses.

In July that year we heard that our patron Michael Denison had died. Michael was the kindest of people, and a true English gentleman. It was he, with John Mills, who had persuaded Sir Alec Guinness to stay with us after the Anneka Rice débâcle.

Then, that September, my dear friend Patricia Hayes, whom I had worked with in childhood and remained close to ever since, lost her long battle against dementia. I thought of all the times Pat had driven up to the Trust to see us, sleeping in the car park in the depths of winter in her tiny camper van, so as not to be a nuisance. We'd had a lifetime of broadcasting and travelling together and for me this was a devastating loss.

More unexpectedly, not long after the Mark Knopfler concert, Ian Bannen was killed in a car crash near Loch Ness. And then a year or two later Michael Williams, Judi Dench's beloved husband of 30 years, the nicest of men and the finest of actors, died at the age of only 65 from cancer. Until his illness Michael had been a regular helper at the Trust. It seemed the whole acting profession was at his memorial service at Covent Garden.

If the Good Lord is casting a play up there in heaven, He's certainly got a hell of a cast to choose from.

Chapter 19

The loss of all these magnificent people suddenly made me feel very vulnerable. I felt life was dangling on such a fine thread that the end could come to any of us, any day.

For a while I became unhealthily introverted and retrospective. I found myself retreating from the realities of the present day to immerse myself in memories of the 'good old days' when life seemed to be all fun and adventure. I thought incessantly of times past, of people long gone, of secure family life.

The horrors of what some people were capable of doing to donkeys didn't help me to feel any more positive about life. The police would relate how young lads had inflicted horrific injuries to animals brought to us for care. These thugs would persecute dumb creatures because they had failed at school, taken drugs or got drunk and felt the need to take their anger out on something that couldn't fight back. Thank God most youngsters are only too pleased to love and care for our animals.

It was the donkeys who jolted me out of this self-indulgent introspection. They needed me in the present day, working for them and for the Trust. I pushed aside my morbid thoughts and dragged myself back to reality.

Chapter 20

By royal appointment

Annie's mother Betty wasn't one to play the couch potato. Her idea of a leisurely stroll was to nip up Ben Cruachon and down again in time for tea. No wonder Annie and her sister Linda were brought up to enjoy walking.

Now Annie wanted to put her love of Shanks' Pony to good use. She suggested that we should stage three long-distance walks with teams of donkeys and children, to raise funds for the Trust.

We decided to start with a 300-mile coast-to-coast walk from Scarborough to Blackpool, with five donkeys, five children and Boo, our Airedale. Yorkshire Television agreed to sponsor it and make a documentary.

The Women's Institutes kindly solved the problem of accommodation for the donkeys. They arranged for us to stay each night in a house with a paddock, so the children would have a hot meal and the donkeys a safe pasture.

We spent four months getting the donkeys used to walking long distances on tarmac. This wasn't easy, as there are quite a few things donkeys don't like about roads - double yellow lines, letterboxes, telegraph poles, streams, bridges, crows, cows, horses, bicycle bells, horns, manhole covers, traffic lights, litter bins and lorries, to mention just a few.

Each Saturday Annie would walk up and down Winnet's Pass to get the team fit. On Sundays they would walk through the towns - Bakewell, Matlock, Chesterfield - to get used to the built-up areas.

When the big day came we drove in convoy to Scarborough in two Land Rovers and trailers. The playwright Sir Alan Ayckbourne and his theatre company came down to the beach to wish us all a safe journey. The start was slightly marred by the enthusiasm of the Town Crier, who panicked the donkeys by roaring out a news announcement and clanging his bell. Finally, waved off by a crowd of local schoolchildren with flags, and to the strains of the local brass band, we set off.

Each day began with a coffee morning, laid on by the wonderful ladies of the local WI. Our accommodation ranged from made-up beds in stables to Ripon Cathedral. It was three weeks, two days and 327 miles before we finally walked on to the promenade at Blackpool. Thanks to Annie's training, we didn't have a blister between us.

At Blackpool Town Hall, the Mayor and Mayoress had arranged a civic reception for the kids and staged a celebration of the donkey, for which of course the resort is famous. The donkeys shared their last night with three elephants, two giraffes and a dozen liberty horses.

The next walk was a little more ambitious - the 900-mile trip from Balmoral Castle to Buckingham Palace. My plan was to leave on April 21, the Queen's birthday, and arrive on June 13, her official one, to see the Trooping of the Colour.

We managed to get permission to start off by walking through the grounds of Balmoral. Our two donkeys, Joshua and Tinker, were escorted by Annie and two twelve-year-olds, Holly Smith and Rachel Davies. Annie and the girls would do the walking while I drove ahead each day with the Land Rover and trailer to wait for them at the place where we were to spend the night.

Chapter 20

A company in Mansfield gave me a horsebox to act as a caravan for the donkeys. I managed to lay on some opulent accommodation for our little party, thanks to the generosity of several large hotel groups.

The start at Balmoral Castle was a splendid affair. Joshua and Tinker wore royal jackets specially made by Annie for the occasion, and we were given an escort by the Queen's Major of The Royal Household. June Brown was interviewed by the media and we were served tea and cakes to speed us on our way.

June joined us for the first ten-mile leg to Braemar, through the royal estate. The Scottish Highland air and the peace and serenity were unlike anything we had experienced. When we go to our hotel in Braemar, we found they had arranged a Highland night with June and the girls as guests of honour. Bagpipes and Celtic music resounded until well into the early hours.

The walking was hard, but the scenery more than made up for it. We plodded to Glenshee and Pitlochry, then struck off through the Cairngorms.

Despite all the preparation, the donkeys dug their heels in a few times. When we came to a burn in the mountains above Pitlochry, the donkeys resolutely refused to cross. The resulting diversion took an extra four hours and delayed our arrival until well after midnight.

Walking through the Scottish scenery and the Dales was a magnificent experience - the cities less so. Once we arrived in the English lowlands we began to follow the canals, which was safe as well as good fun.

We finally reached London Zoo and the waiting TV crews eight weeks and three days after leaving Balmoral. We had walked 947 miles. The Savoy Hotel gave us a spectacular last night by putting us up free of charge.

I wondered what on earth we were going to do with the donkeys - until the manager escorted us round to the back of the hotel to be greeted by the sight of the biggest horsebox I had ever seen. As the ramp descended, everything lit up. The donkeys had the free use of a fax, a telephone, a top-of-the-range George Foreman grill, a television, the works, as well as shavings to die for. They were well impressed.

The next morning we set off down the Mall for the last mile of our journey, followed by television crews from as far away as Japan. As we reached the railings of Buckingham Palace, the sentries stood to arms. A Coldstream Guards major asked us to accompany him round to the Royal Mews and into the Quadrangle. We began to wonder what they were planning.

Cavalry officers were working on their horses and tack to prepare for the following day's ceremony. Another officer came across to ask if we would like to see the golden Coronation Coach and the horses in the livery stables. The royal grooms stepped forward to take charge of Joshua and Tinker.

We were then directed around the walls of the palace to be met by a footman, resplendent in tailcoat, white gloves and red waistcoat. What was going on? I heard a bell ring discreetly, and turned round.

Standing before me was Her Majesty the Queen.

I'm afraid I was completely dumbstruck. I simply couldn't get to grips with it. My legs started shaking and I could feel sweat trickling down my back. I knew that if I opened my mouth I would say something stupid, so I just stood frozen to the spot.

"Good morning, Mr Stirling" said Her Majesty. "No coat, no bag, no hat. An informal private audience. I felt I had to see the donkeys and the children who have made such an effort for my birthday."

I managed a "Thank you, Ma'am" and my nose hit the gravel. Annie and the two children, bless them, all curtsied. Even the donkeys looked bemused.

Chapter 20

Sir Robin Janvrin, the Queen's Private Secretary, stepped forward.

"Congratulations Mrs Stirling" he said to Annie. "Her Majesty has finished the dress rehearsal for tomorrow's Trooping of the Colour, so she wanted to spend the short time available with you all, I hope that's all right".

"We are honoured, Your Majesty" I said. I think she recognised that I was definitely a loyal subject – otherwise I wouldn't have devised the walk.

"May I feed your donkeys?" Her Majesty asked. "We have prepared some carrots." Right on cue another footman arrived on the scene, carrying a Queen Victoria commemorative silver salver bearing eight beautifully-washed carrots, all cut into quarters. There was an ER doily underneath them and another over the top.

The footman stood to attention as he offered the Queen this royal dish of carrots. The donkeys' eyes lit up. I'm pleased to say Joshua and Tinker received their regal gift with excellent manners.

Her Majesty asked the girls all about the journey from Balmoral. She said she had flown over our route many times, but had never thought of walking it.

We left the Palace after a private audience of about twenty minutes. The girls' parents were also brought in and introduced to Her Majesty, which thrilled me as much as it did them.

We were all bewildered - none of us could really take it in. It had passed so quickly, yet it meant so much to both of us.

Annie looked at me when we were back in the Royal Mews.

"That was the highlight of your career, wasn't it?" she said. She gave me a long hug.

I sat outside for ages just winding down. I felt a deep regret that I hadn't thought about taking my parents - it would have meant so much to them. For so many years I had been involved in Silver Jubilees, Royal Variety Shows and Golden Jubilees, but it took two donkeys to grant me an audience that I will never forget.

Annie did another walk after that, from Galway Bay in Ireland to Manchester with three donkeys and three children. She found Ireland a joy. The country was beautiful and the hospitality immensely welcoming. The Irish traders kept coming up to us with wads of notes wanting to buy our donkeys, but Annie knew exactly what to say to that.

Chris de Burgh, the Irish singer, helped us with the project, which I had titled '*One more mile to go*' after one of his hits. Chris offered to do two concerts at the Bridgewater Hall in Manchester if we made it, and he kept his word.

Gert & Daisy

A playbill from the late 1960s

Chris De Burgh

Jean Ferguson of Last of the Summer Wine

Lesley Garrett with Muffin the Mule

Bob Monkhouse

Julian Clary

Pam Ayres with Emily

Kathy Staff and Bill Owen with Oliver

Our royal encounter at Buckingham Palace

Michael Williams with donkeys

Mark Knopfler

Eileen Derbyshire (Emily Bishop)

Jane Freeman & Kathy Staff

Chris De Burgh

Edward Fox and Bergerac

Thora Hird and Oliver

Rolf Harris at the Trust

Patricia Hayes with Tufty

Chapter 21

A shared birthday

Turning 60 a few years ago made me reflect on my life and work and on how things have changed in the entertainment business, sometimes for the better, but sometimes very much for the worse.

I miss the show-business greats who captivated us in our millions in the decades after the war - the larger-than-life personalities who entered our homes and our lives. Entertainers like Morecambe and Wise, Bob Monkhouse, Frankie Howerd, Tony Hancock, Danny La Rue and Marti Caine became part of the family. They won their places in our hearts through real talent, honed and polished through years of hard work. Among the singers, I miss the charm and the sheer skill of the true stars, idols like Dusty Springfield, Tom Jones and Matt Monroe, and the glamour and charisma of Cliff Richard, the Beatles and Billy Fury.

I'm afraid too many of today's entertainers simply don't know much about the job. They are often chosen on talent shows and put in the spotlight purely on the strength of their looks and personality. In the pursuit of the all-important teens and twenties audience, youth, beauty and gimmickry triumph over experience.

Behind the scenes, skilled producers have been replaced by technicians, and computerised technology has come to dominate the whole presentation. The end result is superficial and flashy.

On top of this, the reality TV culture has made the process of becoming an entertainer more important than the finished act. As genuine talent and professionalism are slowly squeezed out, so our values are dropping to a level which would once have been undreamed of.

When truly talented and polished dancers take to the ballroom floor, everybody enjoys the spectacle, the colour, the professionalism and the display of sheer skill. Not so when the company brings in dancers who can't dance, just because they are famous for doing something else, or because they've been plucked off the street and so seem 'one of us'.

The news, meanwhile, has become entertainment for the prurient, headlined by war, crime, horror, obscenity and all the human failings which seem to make the modern world go round. I cringe when I hear some of today's journalists and presenters tearing their interviewees apart like gladiators in ancient Rome.

I don't believe the changes in the entertainment industry have done its public image any favours. Many people think it's all about froth and fame, but the truth is that few professions demand such strictness, professionalism and punctuality. When a plumber or a postman, a lawyer or a journalist, a factory worker, even a doctor doesn't show up as expected, his colleagues fill in and the world gets by. If a lead performer doesn't make it to the show on time, everyone else's work comes to naught and hundreds, maybe thousand, of people are disappointed. I'm afraid the discipline I learned in my working life has made me highly intolerant of people who say they will do something, then fail to deliver.

But that's enough griping from me. I don't wish to be negative - I'm just grateful that I was able to enjoy my time in the industry when I could, and then go on to find something so fulfilling for my later years. The opportunity to turn my hand to building an animal charity was heaven sent. Without the friends I made during my time on and behind the stage,

Chapter 21

I could not have made anything like such a success of it.

I shared my 60th birthday with a character who gloriously combined both my passion for the entertainment industry and my love of donkeys. He isn't actually a donkey - but a mule is pretty close.

Muffin the Mule was created by a husband-and-wife team who happened to be great friends of my mother - Jan Bussell and Anne Hogarth. To a five-year-old boy, to be in the presence of the real Muffin back in those innocent years after the war was something pretty special. The houseboat where Muffin lived was a magical place to be. Jan and Anne made that little wooden puppet and his friends Peregrine the Penguin, Sammy the Seal, Oswald the Ostrich, Louise the Lamb and the others so convincing that to me, as to millions of other youngsters, they were real 'people'

The invitations to Dorking, where Muffin was born, were cherished. Jan's daughter Sally was the same age as myself and together we would climb trees, have picnics and jump off the houseboat into the river. Annette Mills, John Mills' sister, who gave Muffin his name and presented him on TV, would be around writing songs for the show. His daughters Hayley and Juliet were regular visitors. Jan and Anne would put on a puppet show each afternoon to try out new sketches and stories on us. That was quite a responsibility, because our response effectively decided what would go into the show and what wouldn't.

As a producer in later life I had many opportunities to include Muffin in shows, and was able to arrange for him to work with many stars of the day, including Morecambe and Wise, Petula Clark and my dear friend Patricia Hayes.

Muffin became our mascot at the Michael Elliott Trust, and when the BBC dusted him off for a fresh series in animated form a few years ago, he returned to entrance the lives of a new generation of young children.

Chapter 21

Mothers and grandmothers who remembered the 1950s and 1960s would bring their children and grandchildren to meet him.

Muffin's 60th birthday celebration was held at The Grosvenor House Hotel in Park Lane with 800 guests from right across the entertainment industry. Hayley Mills, Bill Kenwright and Martin Shaw, David Suchet, June Brown - there was a long list of stars. The casts of three West End musicals appeared to wish Muffin well. The *Strictly Come Dancing* team came along, and the *Ready Steady Cooks* made a sumptuous meal. Chris de Burgh played the grand piano as Muffin clip-clopped in time on the lid. Judi Dench brought on the cake, which was the size of a billiard table. It was a night to remember.

My own 60th birthday was a rather quieter affair. I booked a candlelit table for two for Annie and me at an Italian restaurant in Poynton. I like to think that Muffin was there in spirit. I suppose that modest celebration was a fair reflection of which of us has had more impact in the world of entertainment.

The success my mother and her parents achieved in the theatrical world gave me huge inspiration for my own career. I have tried to follow in their footsteps to keep the family name alive, and perhaps I have enjoyed a little success. I think I at least inherited their determination and persistence. But the days are long gone when one could enjoy the sort of globe-trotting career which they shared.

As a member of a later generation I have certainly been able to tackle a wide variety of entertainment challenges, from West End shows to concerts and television production. There are times, though, when I would love to travel back in time to enjoy the freedom and the variety my parents' and grandparents' generation enjoyed.

Still - I will always have my donkeys.

June Brown

Waiting for admission to the Palace

June, Rolf, Judy Dunlop and children

A candelabra to honour June Brown's work as chairman

June with young visitors

June meets Cherie Blair at Downing Street